History ❧

in the Spotlight

Creative Drama and Theatre Practices for the Social Studies Classroom

History

in the Spotlight

Creative Drama and Theatre Practices for the Social Studies Classroom

Sharon M. Fennessey

HEINEMANN
Portsmouth, NH

Heinemann
A division of Reed Elsevier Inc.
361 Hanover Street
Portsmouth, NH 03801–3912
www.heinemann.com

Offices and agents throughout the world

The author and publisher wish to thank those who have generously given permission to reprint borrowed material:
Excerpts from *His Name Was Martin* and *The Road to Freedom* by Sharon Fennessey. Copyrighted by Sharon Fennessey. Used by permission of Discovery Enterprises, Ltd.

ISBN 0-325-00161-8

Library of Congress Cataloging-in-Publication Data
CIP information is on file at the Library of Congress.

Editor: William Varner
Production: Denise Botelho, Colophon
Production coordinator: Elizabeth Valway
Cover design: Jill Kyle, Kyle Design
Cover photo: Gordon Rowley
Manufacturing: Louise Richardson

Printed in the United States of America on acid-free paper

07 06 05 04 03 VP 2 3 4 5 6

for Claude,
my loving parents,
and
all my fifth grade students
who made this book possible

Contents

Preface

This book began with my first experience teaching in a fifth grade. At the start of the school year, as I tried to get a sense of my new students' interests, I questioned them about which subjects they enjoyed in school. When I mentioned social studies, they groaned, "It's boring!" A fan of history myself, this attitude was disappointing. I became determined to make history exciting, to breathe some life into the past. I found myself being recruited by this emotional outburst, digging in, and saying to myself, "Is that so? Let's see what can be done about this."

As a teacher with a theatre education background, I put my skills to work. I had always been fascinated by famous people of the past and the drama of their lives. How an ordinary person like Harriet Tubman risked her life to rescue so many on the Underground Railroad, considering the danger involved, was, to me, the essence of drama. Wasn't it possible to learn about a particular period of history by becoming people of the past, reliving some of the dramatic moments of their lives, experiencing the problems and actions of real men and women, and ultimately discover the historical concepts involved? The answer proved to be "yes".

I found that creative drama and theatre are powerful teaching tools, and this book was written as a result of successfully integrating them into the social studies curriculum. The terms *creative drama* and *theatre* are meant to be inclusive of a wide range of communicative arts: pantomime, movement, improvisation, scripted drama, oral interpretation, debating, public speaking, readers theatre, storytelling—just about any way we use the human body or voice to creatively communicate ideas to others. These strategies, if integrated thoughtfully into the social studies curriculum, can be the driving force that motivates and excites students, gives them a goal and a framework that supports their research activities as they move toward an understanding of the concepts. The use of drama and theatre practices in the classroom does not exclude the standards that form the social studies framework. Drama is about life, and because of this, it is inclusive of all of the ten themes in the social studies standards. The strategies presented incorporate cooperative learning and integrate language arts, social studies, and the arts. They also take into account the curriculum standards for social studies, the national standards for arts education in theatre, and Gardner's (1983) theory of multiple intelligences.

As a teacher in today's classroom, I can expect to have learners with diverse abilities and learning styles. Taking this into consideration, I tried to model a variety of strategies that meet the needs of multiples intelligences. The classroom teacher can pick the activity that best suits the ability of learners because a wide range of ideas are presented. Not all activities are meant for all students. A teacher who knows the students' individual abilities can be selective, choosing those activities that will challenge but not overwhelm the learners. The book makes clear how a teacher is supposed to go about integrating drama into the social studies curriculum by outlining lessons and giving practical suggestions to make them work. Detailed descriptions of how to put these strategies in place are presented in sections called In the Spotlight. These sections also include suggested assessment strategies and models for implementation. Curriculum references are in the area of American History, but a creative teacher can adapt the strategies presented and apply them to any historical content. Each chapter includes annotated professional resource books as well as a listing of suggested student books.

My goal is to convince teachers of social studies to experiment with the creative drama and theatre practices presented here to meet the needs of the diverse abilities of their students as they explore history. These practices have worked for me and I'm pleased to share them. Using this approach, my students participate enthusiastically in history lessons. As actors portraying people and events of the past, they come to understand circumstances and characters in the context of time and place, getting an in-depth rather than cursory look at a period of history. Their experiences with the subject are challenging and memorable as they attain new concepts and historical understandings. Finally, excitement replaces boredom in the social studies classroom.

Reference

Gardner, H. [1983] 1993. *Frames of Mind*. New York: Basic Books.

History &

in the Spotlight

Creative Drama and Theatre Practices for the Social Studies Classroom

1

Teaching Social Studies Using Creative Drama and Theatre Practices

We were in a large field picking corn, hungry, tired. On one side, a man with a rifle stared at us. On the other side, the overseer cracked the whip. Someone fell, sick I guessed, but not one of us dared to go help him. The heat made us sweat. We sang in low mournful voices, "Hot boiling sun comin' over, huh, and it ain't goin' down . . . ." It was gonna be a long wait 'til the overseer shouted, "Quittin' time!"

This dramatic improvisation took place in my classroom. It was 1835 and we were slaves on the plantation where Frederick Douglass worked. In this same place, we rode on a bus with Rosa Parks, staged a sit-in at an all-white lunch counter, sailed on the Mayflower, debated the issues of the Patriots and Loyalists, and organized a strike against a Lowell mill owner. These types of drama activities are repeated many times during the year as an integral part of my social studies curriculum. I use drama because students get to participate in the past, reliving situations, digging below the surface of words in a book to discover the underlying meaning of an event. In this example of the plantation improvisation, and later during a play about Douglass, the students were immersed in the lives of the slaves, feeling the indignities, the fear, and finally coming to know the meaning of the word slave. One student writes of the experience in this way:

> The play helped me understand how awful slavery was and made me respect all people better. I'm going to try to treat all people nicer, no matter what they are like. I hope many people in the class feel improved in this way.

> Beth, age 10

Why Drama Needs to Be Part of the Social Studies Curriculum

Besides the benefit of leading students to an in-depth understanding of history, the students are excited about learning this way. In the example here, they were motivated to read more about the pre–Civil War time in history. Jon, who played Frederick Douglass, wanted to research plantation life to gather ideas for his character portrayal. Alyssa developed more self-confidence, as did many others, permanently establishing a voice in the class during discussion or drama activities. Self-discipline was exhibited by all, but was especially noticeable in Jimmy, who learned to listen carefully to other actors and his cues. The list goes on. Concentration, responsibility, team cooperation, critical thinking, and problem solving skills are some of the attributes employed when my students are involved in drama. As the year progresses, I observe their growth. They become more self-assured. The greatest satisfaction for me comes from witnessing their joy and enthusiasm while learning this way. The plays, improvisations, debating, theatre games, pantomime, and so on, are an integral and natural part of the communication process. Talking and moving are what children love to do best. It's fun, and children like learning when it's fun.

With Drama and Theatre, the Social Studies Standards Come into Play

During the planning stage for a unit that incorporates the theatre arts, I consider the social studies standards. With an integrated curriculum approach that employs theatre, creative drama, music, dance, art, literature, reading, writing, and history, there is plenty of opportunity to include them. Drama is about life, and because of this, it is inclusive of the ten themes in the social studies standards. How the standards connect with one particular unit of history is detailed in Chapter 6.

Finding the Time for Drama in the Classroom

The use of drama in the classroom is not a new strategy. For years, teachers have been encouraged to use it as a method of developing oral language, the imagination, aesthetics, gross motor skills, and coordination. Teachers often express to me a sincere interest in "doing some drama," recognize its value as a learning medium, but express doubts as to how they can "fit drama in with all the other subjects in the curriculum." I tell them that their skepticism is well founded, because if drama is treated as a separate entity, it is extremely difficult to squeeze into a teacher's busy day, but if drama is thought of as another way for children to learn, as a strategy for teaching history or any other subject, then it can be integrated into the curriculum. Social studies, in particular, lends itself naturally to drama. History is about people of the past experiencing challenges, joys, or disappointments as they were caught up in the events of their time. Drama, too, is about people interacting in a situation with conflict. When the two are combined, the learners become people of the past, reliving the situations, viewing them from the perspective of the individual. It becomes an effective way for children to construct meaning for past events, to expand an awareness of themselves and the world around them.

Drama can be effectively integrated into the social studies curriculum in the same way that we use historical fiction. Students can vividly recall a character from an historical novel (for example, Daniel from *Jump Ship to Freedom*), yet they struggle to remember anything from a textbook concerning the same historical period (in this case, the unsettled times after the American Revolution). What might be the reason? Perhaps they recall the novel because they're involved in the main character's thoughts and feelings. They're concerned about Daniel's conflict over the slavery issue and the writing of the Constitution. As readers they're involved vicariously in the conflict and emotion of the situation. The same is true when performing a dramatic improvisation of a scene from history.

Drama and Theatre Strategies Motivate Students to Learn About the Past

When students are motivated, they can accomplish just about anything. Using drama as a learning strategy incites children to ask "why?". When they begin to build an improvisational scene, based on an historical situation, many questions surface. They want to know why people behaved this way, what forces propelled them into the situation. For example, when I introduced a thematic unit on civil rights that focused on Langston Hughes, students generated a long list of questions after the first improvisational drama. As a stimulus for the drama, I chose a selection from *The Langston Hughes Reader* (1958), in which Hughes describes his most humiliating Jim Crow experience. The questions began as soon as I finished the reading and continued after the class had improvised the scene, recreating the experience described in the read-aloud. They asked, "Why did the cashier do that to him? Why didn't the owner stop her? Why weren't the other customers angry? Wasn't that against the law? Where did he live? When did this take place? Did this happen in all restaurants?" Because of this drama activity, my students were now curious about Jim Crow laws. Research was initiated on this subject, the post–World War I era, and the Harlem Renaissance. With additional background information, students were then able to contribute to the development of plot and characters in a revised and expanded scene of the initial improvisation. Through this process of combining drama and research, which is described in detail in Chapter 3, they were able to discover the impact of Jim Crow laws, and internalize the underlying meaning of discrimination through their immersion into the past event. One student expressed her feelings about learning history in this way when she wrote:

> Learning history is great fun, but becoming history is capturing! Learning history from textbooks can be done, but I assure you, we won't be eager to come to school. Becoming slaves and whites, and learning teamwork was wonderful. I was, and I'm sure others were too, so eager to come to school, I was dreaming it!

Chelsea, age 10

All Types of Learners Feel Success During a Drama/Theatre Experience

With today's diverse student population, I can expect that the children who arrive in my class in September will have a wide range of abilities. Some students cannot read and comprehend a grade-level textbook, and consequently would experience failure if this were the only channel for learning. I spend a good part of my classroom time observing, conferencing, modeling, and instructing college students who are practicing their teaching skills in my classroom. I remind them often how important it is to reach all learners. Most are not quite sure how to do this. They come with clear memories of what school was like for them: They learned by reading textbooks and writing answers to questions. I try to show them that this method has its limitations, and by using a wide range of communicative arts strategies, there is something to meet the needs of everyone. Learning becomes inclusive and all types of learners feel success. These strategies involve the use of creative thinking, problem solving, and decision making. In cooperative groups, children together reach a solution to the problem presented. The dramatic arts, in fact all arts in general, allow the brain to use wide-ranging problem-solving skills. Howard Gardner's *Frames of Mind* (1983) points out that the human mind possesses multiple intelligences. Solving problems involves several of these intelligences at work. His findings also indicate that every student has two or three intelligences (of the seven major ones that he names) that are particularly strong. If I used the textbook as the only instructional method, for example, I would be limiting students to the standard linguistic method (mainly reading, writing, and discussion) as the channel to achieve historical literacy. The arts, however, encompass all of the intelligences: linguistic, logical/mathematical, visual/spatial, kinesthetic, musical, intrapersonal, and interpersonal. They offer students many opportunities for achievement. The memory of a particular boy jumps into my head when I make this statement. He struggled to read, still at a primary level in the fifth grade. When colleagues saw him playing a leading role in a play about Frederick Douglass, they were astounded. "I couldn't believe his performance!" and "I had no idea he was so talented!" were typical comments. The talent was there all along; I just gave him the opportunity to show it, and it was a very satisfying experience for him as well as for me. To illustrate how activities incorporating the seven intelligences might be applied to a social studies topic, I have created a list of those that I've used for a unit exploring slavery and human rights, with Sojourner Truth as the focus. (This unit is described in detail in Chapter 6.)

- Linguistic: Students, writing in the role of Sojourner Truth, create a diary of her days working on the farm as a slave.
- Logical/Mathematical: Students create a living timeline of key personages in the life of Sojourner Truth.
- Visual/Spatial: Students create political cartoons on the abolitionist/slavery issue.
- Kinesthetic: Students learn a typical folk dance of the 1800s, the Virginia Reel.
- Musical: Students learn popular songs of the Civil War era.
- Interpersonal: Students present a full-length play on the life of Sojourner Truth, taking responsibility for all acting roles, scene changes, and the handling of props.
- Intrapersonal: Students participate in an improvisation on the subject of a slave auction. They experience the humiliation of being sold like animals.

These are only a few examples. There were many more activities involving each of the intelligences. As I observe my students carefully, I come to know the activities at which each child excels. Time and time again, the child who is perceived as a failure by his/her peers, suddenly gains respect and prestige as he/she successfully handles a role in a full-length play, an improvisational classroom drama, pantomime, or any other of the varied activities in drama and theatre. This is what all students want, to gain acceptance for who they are, what they can do, to have their ideas valued, and to feel respected by their teacher and peers. If students truly feel that they are being respected, their confidence soars, and they can do just about anything. One of my fifth graders expressed his feelings about his theatre experience in an historical drama in this way:

> I think the play makes everyone feel good about themselves. For a lot of children, the play was a big confidence booster, and it helped the children in the classroom as well as in acting. Now, I know that I can remember my lines, and now I cannot doubt myself at all.
>
> Rocco, age 10

Like drama, history is about people and how they interact with each other, their conflicts, celebrations, and tragedies.

Students Get a Detailed View of History
While Immersed in the Past

Educators as well as students have long criticized history textbooks as uninspiring accounts of events of the past, listing names, dates, places of battles, and so forth. Due to limited space, textbooks often give a brief account of important events, leaving out the heart of the matter, that is, "the humaneness" of the situation. Slowly this is changing as the demand for more inspiring and lively accounts increases. When I use drama with my students in the classroom, we look at an event in detail. I provide background material, often firsthand accounts and biographies, that helps my students get a sense of who these characters from the past were, and how they behaved as important events unfolded, or in everyday life. For example, when I did a unit on the theme of slavery, I read an account of a slave auction written by the slave Solomon Northup (in Meltzer's *The Black Americans: A History in Their Own Words* [1984]). This account gave students a clear picture of how slaves were sold. Through the eyes of Northup, we shared in the fear and humiliation of the slaves, getting a close-up view of this human drama. Through a follow-up improvisational drama, students became people of the past, experiencing their problems as they were caught up in the forces of their time. The historian, Milton Meltzer (1993), notes the importance of establishing common bonds with people from the past when he writes:

> I want the reader to discover what it felt like to be alive at that time. I want the reader to share directly in that experience, to know the doubts, the hopes, the fears, the anger and joy of the men, women, and children who were the blood and bone of that history.

When students in my class immerse themselves, through the dramatic arts, in the lives of people from the past, they get a detailed look at a particular time or event. By doing this, they move toward an understanding of the concepts physically, emotionally, and intellectually. One fifth grader, while assessing the drama experience in class, expressed how it felt to be immersed in someone else's life, in this case Harriet Tubman. For this unit, one of the big ideas I wanted to convey was that slaves were denied their basic constitutional rights. This student seems to have gotten it when she writes:

> Well, acting is like being that person, so you understand it more when the master or mistress says, 'You'll be punished!' It's not like being grounded by your parents and not watching TV. It's like being whipped, physical punishment, and knowing how some people back then could think that blacks were like animals, or less than human. I got the feeling of what it was like, almost like being in their shoes.

Kayla, age 10

Drama Encourages an Understanding and Expression of Multiple Points of View

Kayla, playing the role of the slave, certainly got a feel for what it was like, but what about Alex, the student who played the role of the master? How did he feel? He had to explore what motivated these men to work their slaves relentlessly (the other side of the slavery issue). He writes about his character this way:

> I am a slave overseer, a harsh, non-understanding man.
>
> Alex, age 10

Having to assume the roles of a variety of characters, it became important for all students to see this time in history from more than one perspective, discover some insight into the feelings of those who were pro-slavery, fighting to keep the plantation system going, as well as the abolitionists who wanted to free the slaves. Another student, Chloe, writes of her experience:

> In a history textbook, you normally just get the facts. By doing the play, my class learned everybody's point of view on slavery: the plantation owners, the overseers, the abolitionists, and the slaves. Doing a play also helped me visualize what it was truly like in that time in history. By seeing the cruelty of the master to the slave (in the play), we not only learned that the master was cruel to his slave, but we truly understood and realized the cruelty.
>
> Chloe, age 10

By using drama as a teaching strategy, I felt that students could understand not only that our daily lives present us with problems that require an understanding of multiple points of view, but that history is filled with situations in which the people involved had multiple perspectives. Certainly, the American colonists were at odds as to whether they should declare independence from England. When we study this conflict in class, students see that there are valid arguments to support more than one point of view. Once they understand that there are other positions, they are better able to empathize with the opposition. Understanding and empathy, I felt, were desirable qualities for both students and teachers.

Historical Drama Evokes an Aesthetic Response to Events, Connecting the Past to the Present

By stepping into events of the past through the dramatic arts, the learners begin to identify with the characters being portrayed, and share in their feelings. The aesthetic response can take many forms, such as an activity in movement, pantomime, improvisation, oral interpretation, or writing in role. Gradually, students begin to make sense of what these people lived through, deepening their understanding of how they coped with a particular situation. Jason, who played the role of a slave catcher in the Harriet Tubman drama, responds to the historical experience this way:

> A play is different from a book because in a book, you read the information, but you can't read feeling. In a play, the feeling is the most expressed thing. A play gives you a different point of view. You're still just an observer, but you can feel how cruel slavery was and the terrible conditions on the plantation.

Jason, age 10

To help students bring to life these stories of the past, I find that it is important to read original documents left behind by these people. Primary sources, such as letters, journals, newspapers, diaries, and so on, reveal what people were thinking and feeling at that time. By examining these records of past generations (through read-alouds, videotapes, audiocassettes, for example), children come to understand that humans, living in the past or in the present, are motivated by the same basic emotions and share traits common to all humankind. Every child can make the connection between the cruelty of an overseer of slaves and the cruelty of someone they have known or have heard of in their own life, perhaps the schoolyard bully.

Critical Thinking and Creative Problem Solving Are Promoted

The complexities of an historical event and the idea of varying perspectives are the basis for an historical knowledge which students can apply to the world around them. Through drama activities, students learn to analyze problem-solving situations and apply what they know to make decisions where there are no standard answers. When my students assume a role in an historical event, they quickly realize, after the issues have been raised, that there is more than one perspective to be considered, and that not all problems have only one answer. This is the perfect atmosphere for the creation of an improvisational drama. As students play out scenes from different points of view, they recognize, just as in their own lives, that there is more than one side to every situation. The complexities of history are made apparent. As an example, I'll cite a scene we improvised during our study of the American Revolution, "The Boston Massacre and the Aftermath" (see Chapter 3). Testimony given by the British captain contradicted the testimony presented by the members of the Boston mob. Both sides were sincere in their convictions. Students were impressed by the complexity of the situation, and this led them to consider varying solutions to the problem of who should be blamed for the massacre, and they realized that these types of situations are not uncommon in history, or in everyday life.

To engage students in meaningful dramatic improvisations, based on events from the past, they must have sufficient background knowledge. To assure that this happens, I provide students with a variety of resources that will allow them to enter into the event, to become the person of the past, and to make informed decisions as they plan their scenes. The type of humanizing details that students need will not be found in a history textbook. Instead, I make available a variety of resource materials, including historical fiction, well-written nonfiction, and primary documents, which provide detailed information for the learners as they investigate the past.

The Dramatic Arts Integrate Easily into All Facets of Classroom Learning

The use of drama as a strategy is a natural way to learn. Children are involved in hands-on experiences, doing what most enjoy best—talking and moving. The integrated curriculum, which incorporates the arts, humanities, and the sciences, is a reflection of the real world, where learning occurs through interrelated experiences. Language arts and social studies, in particular, are intertwined, enhancing each other as a drama project unfolds during an integrated unit of study.

While studying a particular period of history, I provide opportunities for my students to explore events, framed in the context of society and its culture. It's hard to imagine, for example, when we studied the Civil Rights Movement of the 1950s and 1960s, not to include some of the freedom songs connected with the movement. In Chapter 6, which gives an in-depth look at one particular project, you'll see that social studies is integrated into other content areas, and dance, music, and the visual arts are an integral part of the theatre activities.

This is also true of history. It naturally includes the arts; it's not a contrived situation. The arts were and are the expression of a particular culture and time, so logically they should be included in a study of history.

The Arts, Especially Drama/Theatre, Prepare Students for the Real World and the Workplace

A common complaint voiced by business and corporate leaders is that many young people in today's workforce lack responsibility and discipline and cannot communicate effectively. Communication, responsibility, and discipline can be nurtured through the dramatic arts. All the arts, in fact, promote social growth.

I've witnessed, time and again, students who gain confidence in front of an audience because they regularly have the opportunity to practice oral language. I've observed significant growth in written language, especially fiction and research writing, because it is more purposeful and motivated. Learners are eager to research when preparing a news show script, for example. They try to present stories accurately and keep the material stimulating, knowing that they will perform them in front of an audience.

They work responsibly in groups and as individuals. I've observed ten-year-old children backstage take responsibility for moving scenery quickly, quietly, and on time. I've watched with great satisfaction as students cue each other for entrances, or remind another actor about a prop. Such activities encourage children to look beyond themselves and see their connectedness to others as part of a team. They learn to listen carefully, engage constructively in an exchange of ideas, and respect opposing points of view. This is obvious in debate activities or in the simulation of a town meeting. As their knowledge of self increases, their sensitivity and understanding of others increases. I've observed countless instances of students who entice a shy child into a scene by using encouraging words.

During creative drama or a theatrical presentation, students learn to assess problems in their work and find appropriate solutions. They meet deadlines and conduct themselves in a disciplined manner at rehearsals and during in-class projects. Although excitement and enthusiasm abound, kids sense the need to waste as little time as possible as the team prepares to share its work in front of an audience.

Consider, as illustration, the example of a student who entered my fifth grade with the reputation of being undisciplined, disruptive, and uncooperative throughout his years at school. No student wanted this child on their team. Then one day he created a convincing, hilarious pantomime that solved the problem presented in the drama session. From then on, in group scenes, he was in demand and his ideas were accepted among the participants. A talent emerged that was not evident in tasks that focused mainly on reading and writing. As he gradually gained acceptance in the class, his position in the group changed and he was treated with respect by his peers. With the feeling of being respected and accepted, he developed confidence in himself. Later that year, he was able to handle one of the major roles in a scripted historical play. He cooperated both on and off stage during the production, assuming responsibility as part of the team and recognizing the importance of teamwork.

What took place is not uncommon. The arts, especially drama, bring out the best in children as they interact, working toward a common goal. One fifth grade student expressed his ideas on this subject in a most straightforward way:

> I learned that you need to set aside you differences and work as a team to accomplish your objective, respect each other, and not fool around. I learned that I could act and be someone who I am not. I also could work with my enemies without killing them.

Tom, age 10

Another student expressed similar feeling about the importance of working together:

> I learned quite a bit about teamwork. For instance, our class could not do the play if there were little groups or cliques of people. The only way we could make a play great was if we had teamwork, something our class gradually accomplished.

Elizabeth, age 10

Drama promotes social growth in the classroom, in the school community, and in the real world by giving children an opportunity to work cooperatively toward a common goal, and to develop confidence, discipline, an understanding of self, and sensitivity to others.

The Final Argument for Using Drama and Theatre to Teach Social Studies

Probably the most important reason I use creative drama and theatre in the classroom is that children get excited about it. Most of us, as teachers, at the beginning of the year, take the time to observe our students as individuals. We gather information about ways in which they learn best, and then we choose learning strategies to meet their needs. The arts accommodate the needs of diverse learning styles. Students are engaged in self-expression, making discovery possible. They get to participate in their own learning. As one student expressed earlier in this chapter, they can't wait to come to school because they're excited about what's happening in the classroom.

Resources

Selected Professional Resources

Cecil, N.L. & P. Lauritzen. 1994. *Literacy and the Arts for the Integrated Classroom: Alternative Ways of Knowing*. White Plains, NY: Longman. This book is organized into three parts. Part One discusses the importance of using the arts as a learning medium. Part Two suggests ways in which the theory can move into practice when using an integrated approach. Part Three presents ideas for encouraging an appreciation of the arts. There is also an extensive bibliography of children's literature about the arts.

Gardner, H. [1983] 1993. *Frames of Mind*. New York: Basic Books. In this book, Gardner explains his theory of multiple intelligences, which challenges the idea that intelligence is a single general capacity, varying in degrees in each individual. The 1993 edition has an introduction that explores the theory's development during the previous ten years.

McCaslin, N. 1996. *Creative Drama in the Classroom and Beyond*, 6th ed. White Plains, NY: Longman. This is an excellent reference, as it covers all facets of creative drama for the classroom and performance for an audience. Chapters include movement, pantomime, improvisation, puppetry, building plays, using poetry, storytelling, speech activities, and scripted drama. This book is well organized, easy to follow, and filled with practical ideas.

References

Collier, J.L. & C. Collier. 1981. *Jump Ship to Freedom*. New York: Delacorte.

Douglass, F. [1845] 1968. *The Narrative of the Life of Frederick Douglass*. New York: Signet.

Graves, D. 1989. *Experiment with Fiction*. Portsmouth, NH: Heinemann.

Hughes, L. 1958. *The Langston Hughes Reader*. New York: George Braziller.

Meltzer, M. 1993. "Voices from the Past." In *The Story of Ourselves: Teaching History Through Children's Literature*, eds. M.O. Tunnell & R. Ammon, 27–30. Portsmouth, NH: Heinemann.

———. [1964] 1984. *The Black Americans: A History in Their Own Words*. New York: HarperCollins.

National Council for the Social Studies. 1994. *Curriculum Standards for Social Studies: Expectations for Excellence*. Washington, DC: National Council for the Social Studies.

2

Setting the Stage for Learning

I think almost the entire class, including myself, learned about working with each other. We may not have liked each other, but we were all people trying to put on a play. The play kind of made all the problems, like teasing that us girls would fight over, seem so small.

Brook, age 10

When a new class of fifth graders arrives in September, I spend time observing them carefully in work and play situations, trying to assess their social development. I have learned, as I'm sure other teachers have, that unless the social skills are in place, the chances of a classroom functioning as a successful place for learning are practically nil. This is especially true of children in the middle grades. They lack confidence and spend a lot of time and energy trying to look "cool" for their peers. In a classroom where drama and theatre strategies are used, a positive social atmosphere is essential. Much of the year in my class is spent in collaborative group work, so developing a sense of community, trust, and shared responsibility becomes a primary goal for me.

Focusing on Social Skills Helps Set the Stage for Learning

I start with a discussion of the most essential ingredient for any successful classroom, that is, mutual respect. Students need to respect each other, and as a teacher, I need to respect and accept each student for who they are and where they are in their academic and social development. I try to make the classroom a safe place where everyone feels secure enough to try out an idea. My students, when participating in a drama session, for example, know that their peers will not laugh, but rather respect their effort to solve the problem at hand. This doesn't happen magically. I spend a lot of time developing a sense of community and mutual respect. It is not an easy task, and it's a constant struggle to maintain it throughout the year, but practice helps. By practicing in a series of drama activities aimed at building group awareness, confidence, cooperation, and concentration, students will improve.

My behavior is also a key factor. To promote the idea of respect, I model it. I try to be supportive, encouraging, and handle negative behavior in a positive manner. For example, when one of my students engages in "horseplay" to get attention during a social studies/drama activity, my response might be something like this: I ask the student to recall the problem or task that was explained at the outset of the session. Then I ask the student to describe his or her response to the problem. As I ask a series of questions designed to help the student self-evaluate, it becomes evident to the student that the horseplay was not a valid response to the problem presented. By handling negative behavior in this way, the focus is put on the activity rather than on the child's behavior. I then give the student a chance to rethink the response and come up with an alternative solution. By doing this, I've demonstrated that I respect what was offered, but I've also helped the student discover that the response was not an appropriate solution to the problem. By modeling this behavior frequently in drama sessions, soon other students use the same approach to evaluate their work and others by recalling the original problem and assessing whether the response was a legitimate attempt to find a solution. Gradually the students approach drama seriously, viewing it as another part of their daily learning. There are lapses, of course, but if the majority behave positively, then others will follow, because they all want to be accepted in the class community.

I cannot emphasize enough the importance of setting the stage for learning by giving time and attention to social skills. Persistence is important. It takes time and patience to stop an activity and deal with inappropriate behavior. But the time is well spent. When I've tried to save time and move on, ignoring the horseplay, it persists and interferes later on with the drama activity. The success of using creative drama and theatre practices in the social studies classroom is dependent on learners who can work as an ensemble or in collaborative groups. I have discovered during years of experimentation that this approach works only if there is a reciprocal flow of information between its participants in an atmosphere of respect and trust.

Making Expectations Clear

Like most teachers, at the start of the school year, I make my expectations clear for social and academic performance. I expect high standards from all. These are just words to the newcomers. As the students hear them, I can almost see the thoughts racing through their heads, "There she goes with the usual first-day-of-school speech . . . ." These words take on meaning only when they're put into practice. Because I have a reputation as the "teacher who does drama," when kids arrive in my fifth grade, they mistakenly think that it's time for horseplay and skits. After a few sessions in our drama circle, trying to meet the challenges presented in a social studies/drama activity, they begin to recognize that discipline, concentration, risk taking, hard work, and organization are all necessary in drama, just as they are in the other academic areas.

The same high standards apply to me as well. Modeling the attributes I expect from the learners stresses their importance. To create a productive social studies classroom, I carefully plan drama activities with curriculum content in mind. I organize blocks of time to accomplish our goals, and prepare supporting resource material. I share my evaluation criteria with the students, putting it on the overhead projector and discussing each item.

We begin each creative drama or theatre session with a shared purpose. Experiencing these activities almost daily, students gradually begin to view drama as another way to learn, and their visions of the day-long "drama recess" begin to fade.

Creating a Backdrop for Reflective Learners

I let students know that drama has a place in the classroom by creating a space where the class can meet as a group, *the drama circle area*. It is large enough for all students to meet comfortably for discussion or to listen to directions. It is a place for group improvisation, read-alouds, storytelling, presentations, or scene rehearsals. The area has a prop (or property) shelf, some costume pieces, and some all-purpose furniture available for students to use, as needed, in their work. Props can be kept very simple—a few dishes, cups, magazines, newspapers, a briefcase, cane, or eyeglasses. For costume pieces, a few hats of varying styles, purses, shawls, aprons, and capes are examples that might be useful. Other work areas, with large tables at various places around the room, allow space for small groups to plan and prepare their work.

Collections of *reference materials* that I've gradually built up during preceding years are also located around the room. For general reference, there is a shelf with dictionaries, encyclopedias, history texts, atlases, and a timeline book. A second area, next to the computers, has relevant CDs; a third area, which changes according to the current unit of study, contains an assortment of fiction and nonfiction books, copies of primary documents, maps, and cassette tapes of folk songs, photocopies of historical images, photos, and a bibliography listing books that might serve as a reference.

A variety of *resources outside the classroom* also help enrich the students' learning. There is a space on the bulletin board for local arts and museum news. I post articles (and encourage students to do the same) on children's theatre, dance groups (especially folk dance), and exhibits of art and photography that pertain to history. Our field trips include experiences in the arts and living history museums.

Figure 2–1. Working in the Drama Circle

On occasion, actors who portray the role of historical people visit the class. This allows students to see and interact with a professional actor in role. Use of storytellers is another way to enrich students' experience and develop their interest in using drama as a learning medium. I have found that parents, grandparents, friends, and local personalities are an accessible and inexpensive resource. They are a wealth of information, giving firsthand accounts of recent historical events or time periods. At times, we've heard fascinating accounts of the experience at home and on the battlefront during World War II.

Another effective way to enhance the learning atmosphere is for me to *show enthusiasm for the subject matter*. Enthusiasm is contagious. When I'm excited about trying a new activity in creative drama, for example, or sharing something I've discovered while researching a person in history, the attention of my students is caught. They become curious and want to participate in discovering something new of their own. To generate and keep the enthusiasm going, I've used some of the following ideas:

- I participate with the students in an improvisation or pantomime.
- I work along with a group of students to stage a reader's theatre.
- I read or tell a story about a dramatic event or detailed first-person account in history.

- I write a script for a scene developed in class.
- I visit the historical society to find the local connection to the unit being studied.
- I borrow artifacts or primary documents to share with the class.

Finally, to create a setting that encourages reflective learning, I find that it is important for me to *be a skilled listener*. This contributes greatly to any classroom, especially for those teachers engaged in writing or reading conferences. Teachers who are good listeners focus on the possibilities for helping students by asking questions. Whether in a one-on-one conference, a collaborative group, or an entire class discussion, I need to be prepared to ask thought-provoking questions that assist students in discovering approaches or solutions to the problems presented. In a drama activity, for example, I listen and watch critically. When an improvisation is finished, I ask questions that will help students evaluate the scene and develop it further. This is not easy to do. I've been working on my questioning skills for years and it's still a constant struggle to formulate the right question for a given situation.

Planning an Interdisciplinary Unit

To integrate drama and theatre activities successfully into social studies learning, I carefully plan the unit, considering the needs of my students. Materials for use in the classroom are gathered ahead of time and books are reserved in the school library. I think about the overall theme as well as the concepts to be presented. (See Figure 6–1 in Chapter 6 for a sample unit overview.) When choosing fiction and nonfiction material, I keep the diverse abilities of the learners in mind. I decide whether the class is sufficiently skilled to conduct research. If not, I plan a series of minilessons to model a variety of skills, such as finding information, note taking, visual techniques for recording and organizing information, formats for recording research findings, and written responses to literature studied in class. Students are encouraged to develop organizational skills, recording information in a spiral-bound notebook, which is used during the year as a portfolio of individual learning. I outline clearly what needs to be done, including intermediary and final due dates for assignments. I emphasize research to go hand in hand with the historical drama experience. Students have difficulty creating believable dramatic situations without knowing the historical background. With this type of experiential learning, they immerse themselves in the past, but they need to develop a strong knowledge base to be successful living there.

I carefully choose the arts activities for an integrated unit to enhance the social studies content, keeping in mind my students' particular interests and talents. Visual arts, music, dance, and drama are part of the social studies classroom experience.

These activities help the learners develop a cultural sense of a particular era. I incorporate folk dance and music because they express the thoughts and feelings of ordinary people at the time. For example, plantation work songs were a part of a unit on slavery. Artwork is sometimes practical (as in the form of scenery, props, and graphic design), or an activity that gives insight into the culture from which it originated.

With an integrated unit, I schedule large blocks of uninterrupted time for research, meeting with cooperative groups, drama activities, literature discussions, minilessons, viewing videos, listening to read-alouds, or writing. In a self-contained classroom such as mine, I easily schedule all the activities. In a team-teaching situation, scheduling integrated activities is more challenging, but possible. With advance planning, a social studies/drama/language arts unit can be worked into the curriculum. Including specialists in the planning stage helps to make it a truly integrated project.

Finally, while planning the unit, I consider how to interest my students in the topic, to initiate a discussion and a generous flow of questions. Examples of motivating activities are a read-aloud, a videotape with dramatically presented content, a primary document, an artifact, or a guest speaker. During a study of World War II and the Holocaust, for example, I used several guest speakers. They related their war experiences to the class. One grandfather told of the realities of ground warfare on a Pacific Island. Another speaker, of Jewish heritage, gave an account of the horrors of his deportation from Germany to a work camp in Siberia, where most of his family perished.

I've found that careful planning of an integrated unit is crucial to the success of learning through the medium of drama and theatre. Chapter 6 details the specifics of planning, organizing, and carrying out an integrated social studies/drama/language arts project on the topic of slavery.

Activities That Prepare Students for Learning Through the Medium of Drama and Theatre

At the outset of the year, I spend time developing what I call the *3 C's: confidence, cooperation,* and *concentration.* On this framework of attributes I build extensive projects, such as full-length plays, a living museum, or reenactments. Without developing these as a foundation, I've learned that experiencing history through drama and theatre is on shaky ground. Progress is slow and results are without substance. I start off with a variety of simple activities that lay the foundation for more complicated, challenging ones. By spending the first six to eight weeks on these activities, the students get to know and trust each other, becoming more willing to take risks while in drama circle. I observe them, making mental notes on individual behaviors. They learn how I run a drama activity, know my routines and expectations. They gradually develop skills in pantomime, learning how to move with precision when needed. These experiences also provide practice in oral language.

The following sample activities are designed to help children develop the ability to work together as a team, not be shy or show off while working on drama, and attend carefully to the problem presented in the lesson. Many of the activities are traditional theatre or children's games. Some have been adapted to focus on history, others have not. For those activities with no history focus, you might ask yourself, "What does this have to do with teaching social studies?" My answer is this: I've observed over the years that children need to have social skills in place and feel secure working with their peers before they are able to function as a productive class. These activities promote individual development and an awareness of one's identity (theme IV of the social studies standards) and prepare children for learning through the medium of drama and theatre.

A sampling of games and activities is listed here, but for a more extensive repertoire of activities, you might refer to one of the educational drama books listed in Resources at the end of this chapter.

Introductions (a get-acquainted activity for the entire class)

All players stand in a circle, and I choose a leader. The leader starts the game by saying his or her name, then makes a gesture or movement. (Example: The player says her name, "Marilyn," then makes a "stop" gesture with her arm, repeating it right and left several times.) The whole group repeats the name, "Marilyn," and imitates the gesture suggested by the player. One by one, the players each say their names, then create a gesture or movement, which the entire group repeats. The game continues until all players have had a turn.

Who Started the Motion? (a concentration/observation game for the entire class)

In this traditional game, players stand in a circle. One player is sent from the room, and another player is chosen to be the leader. The leader begins an action, which all the players imitate. The player who was sent outside returns, takes a place in the center of the circle, and begins to observe the group, trying to guess who is leading the motions. When the center player guesses correctly, the game begins again with a new player chosen to go outside. (Through discussion, I help students develop strategies for watching the leader without making it obvious.)

Talk Show Host (a partner activity to develop confidence)

I divide players into pairs. Everyone interviews his or her partner with a set of predetermined questions. (Examples: What are your favorite summer activities? What events in history interest you? Where do you live?) Partners then utilize the information gathered in the interview to create an introduction for their partner. Each player takes a turn being the "host" and introducing the person to the entire group. (I limit the interview to five or six questions for this introductory activity. Each introduction takes about thirty seconds. I encourage students to speak in a clear, loud voice to communicate their information to the audience.)

Mystery Bag (an entire class activity to develop confidence)

I tell students to bring to school a bag (a brown paper lunch or grocery bag works well) in which three objects (either real or symbolic) have been placed. I tell them that these three objects are things that they would like to have with them if they were to be marooned on a deserted island in the middle of the ocean. They should assume that their basic needs for food, clothing, and shelter are met (no survival items needed). Examples might be a book, some candy, and a fishing rod. Each student in the drama circle takes a turn showing the objects and explaining why these objects were chosen. Encourage students to speak in clear, complete sentences, introducing each object in a logical order (if necessary) and finishing with a short conclusion. (Another version of this activity, called *Artifacts*, uses objects with historical significance.)

Tasting Imaginary Foods (a pantomime activity for partners or small groups, good for developing concentration and building confidence)

I divide the class into small groups or partners. Each group selects a card at random from a pile of cards. On each card I have printed the name of a food. Each group plans *where* they are (a setting) when eating the food, then they perform the pantomime together. For example, if a group selects a card that says "popcorn," they might decide to be "at the movies" as their "where." They line up some chairs and perform the pantomime. I encourage each group to concentrate on showing the size, shape, texture, taste, temperature, and personal feelings about the food. I coach them to reveal their "where" or setting through their pantomime actions. Here is a sample list of foods and the settings created by my fifth grade students:

The Food	The "Where"
hot dog	baseball park
pizza	school cafeteria
marshmallows	around a campfire
ice cream	at the beach
french fries	in a car
peanut butter sandwich	watching TV
sour apple	in an orchard
watermelon	at a school picnic

Talk Show Host II

This activity has an historical focus and requires several days' preparation time. It is a more advanced activity and would best be done after several months of learning through drama.

I divide the players into groups of five or six. Each player picks a name card from a prepared pile. Each card gives the name of a person connected to the historic period being studied in class. The players must then research and prepare autobiographical information on the character chosen. One player in the group is chosen as "the host" and the other players are "the guests" on the talk show. After announcing the guests' names, the talk show host asks questions and calls on members of the audience, who direct their questions at the famous individuals.

Version 2

In this activity, I ask the players to create their own historical identities (examples: a member of the mob in the Boston Massacre, a servant at the First Continental Congress, a soldier in the British army during the American Revolution). The host of the show does not introduce the guests. Instead, the audience asks questions to determine the identity of the mystery guests on the talk show.

The Magic Rope (a large group pantomime to develop cooperation and concentration)

I place a rope on the floor in the center of the drama circle. On a signal from me, everyone picks up the rope and creates the shape I call out. For example, if the I call out "square," the players create a square shape with the rope, then walk it around the room keeping the square shape, or lifting it up and down, all the while concentrating on maintaining the shape. Other shapes might be rectangle, trapezoid, parallelogram, triangle, and so forth. I tell students to focus on making the group movements as smooth as possible. Group cooperation is a *must* for this activity. Note: I have found that this activity is more successful with "side coaching" (a term used in drama to refer to the coaching done by the leader to guide the students through the interaction as they work to stay focused and solve the problem presented). I call out words, phrases, or questions to guide the students. For example, in *The Magic Rope,* I might say, "Keep its shape! Take your time! How can you move the shape as one?" (For more on side coaching, see Chapter 3.)

Pass the Object (a large group pantomime to develop concentration and cooperation)

All students stand in a circle, and I begin by passing an imaginary object around the circle. I start with an object that is familiar to children. Examples are a basketball, a balloon, a small bouncing ball, a feather, and so on. I try to make the chosen object clear to the players by using it in some way (for example, dribbling a basketball). I direct the students to take the object, use it in some way, and then pass it on. As the imaginary object moves around the circle, it is important that the players focus on its physical properties, especially its size, shape, and weight. I suggest to the players that they concentrate on their pantomime actions because they may be asked to repeat the actions at another time. After passing the imaginary object around the circle several times, I use the real object (for example, a basketball). Then I direct the students again to concentrate on the size, shape, weight, and their handling of it as they repeat the same actions they created with the imaginary object. After the real object has made several trips around the circle, I take the object away and pass an imaginary one once more. This time, a significant improvement in the accuracy of the pantomime is noticed.

Who Am I? (a large group activity that promotes concentration and cooperation, suggested to be done following research of an historic period)

Before the activity, I prepare name cards of people from the historic period we studied in class. (For example, if the time period was World War II, I might include such names as Franklin D. Roosevelt, Winston Churchill, Jesse Owens, Eleanor Roosevelt, Adolf Hitler, Mussolini, Marian Anderson, Charles Lindbergh, Albert Einstein, etc.). I divide the class into large groups of six to eight students. To each student's back I tape a name card, being careful not to let the student see the name. Players, taking turns in the group, ask questions to determine their identity. Only questions that can be answered with a "yes" or "no" response are allowed. (Possible sample questions: Am I a woman? Am I in politics? Am I married to a famous person? Am I married to a president? etc.) The questioning continues until all players know their identity.

This Is Your Life (a large group pantomime activity; works well as a lead-in to scenes with dialogue)

For this activity, I read a picture book biography, or I tell a story of a famous person from history. Afterward, I lead a discussion focusing on the important events in the person's life. We list them chronologically on chart paper. I divide the class into five or six groups, depending on how many events are listed on the chart paper, and then assign each group an event. Each group plans a pantomime that reveals information about that phase of the person's life. An example of a fifth grade experience with this activity is as follows: I read a story about Magellan's adventures as an explorer. Some of the exciting events in his life were listed on chart paper. Students pantomimed a dramatic moment from each event. One group mimed the boat's crew, weak from starvation, cooking and eating leather in the absence of food. Another group mimed the wounding and death of Magellan during a battle with the natives on a Philippine island.

Expressing Feelings (a large group movement/mime activity with an historical focus)

A read-aloud is a good springboard for this activity. I choose something that expresses great emotion. Letters, journals, first-person narrative, and poetry are good choices (see Resources at the end of this chapter). An example for a unit on slavery is *Letters from a Slave Girl,* by Mary E. Lyons. After reading a dramatic section, I discuss the general feeling conveyed by the reading, asking the students to think about a time when they have experienced similar feelings, such as fear, anger, sadness, or helplessness. Then I tell the players to stand in a circle, facing out. This helps players concentrate. I direct them to think about the feeling that we discussed in the reading. If the feeling is *sadness,* I might coach them as follows:

> Show the sadness in your face, your eyes, your eyebrows, your mouth, your whole head. Let your shoulders be sad, your arms. Feel the sadness in your legs, your feet. Now turn to your right and begin to walk around the circle. Show the sadness in your walk. How can you show the sadness with your feet? Now concentrate on showing the sadness with every part of your body.

Artifacts (an individual activity that is good for developing confidence, because players take on the role of historians)

At the outset of the year, students explore the question, "How do historians find out about the past?" One resource, they discover after brainstorming, is the artifact. I ask each student to bring one object in a brown bag: a letter, a photo, a document, or something that has historical significance in the family. (I give examples of items passed down from one family to another, or brought to this country when a family immigrated, etc.) I tell them to be prepared to speak about the object, knowing its approximate age, origin, and what it reveals about the past. Usually, a wide variety of objects appear in drama circle: photos of grandparents or great grandparents, a war medal, a birth certificate, old coins, ration coupons from World War II, a wedding veil, an army uniform hat, a watch, a bowl, a cloth covered box, a doll, an immigration card, and so forth.

Artifacts II (a pantomime activity that helps to develop concentration)

I arrange players to work with a partner. After students participate in *Artifacts,* the objects can be used to suggest characters for a pantomime activity. Those artifacts that are not too fragile and that students have volunteered to share are put in the center of the drama circle where all students can see them. I ask students to visually pick an object; then I tell them that they will be asked to take that object from the center of the circle and react to it in the role of a particular character. For example, one student in my class picked up a war medal, and acting in the role of an army officer, mimed ceremoniously pinning it on another student, who assumed the role of a soldier. Two other students in the class picked up the same medal, assumed the role of children, and mimed finding the medal in a trunk in the attic, looking at it curiously.

Artifacts III (improvisational drama for small groups, suggested for students who have had some experience with improvisational drama as described in Chapter 3)

The artifacts that were brought by students (see *Artifacts*) are put in the center of the circle. They are used to suggest a scenario for an improvised scene. To model the idea of creating a scene from an artifact, I usually pick one object and ask students to make up a story about it. Sometimes the idea for a scene has already been suggested from the information given by the student who brought the artifact to school. (In this example, I chose some old coins from the pile of artifacts. Together we made up the following situation for a scene: A family is being forced to move out of their apartment because they haven't paid the rent. They are all packing their belongings. While packing, one of the children finds a shoebox pushed way back on the top shelf of a closet. In the box are the old coins. The family wonders if they are valuable. The father takes the coins to a dealer and finds out that they are valuable. The coins are sold, and the family is able to pay their bills and stay in the apartment.) Once the scenario is created, I call on students to act out the different parts of the scene.

Advanced Version of Artifacts III

After the idea of creating a scene from artifacts is modeled and the students have had experience with creating improvisational scenes (as detailed in Chapter 3), I divide the class into groups of four to five students. Each group is then asked to pick one of the artifacts and make up a scene about it. Usually, I have them start the planning in the first session, then complete the planning and performing of the scene during the following session. The artifacts, along with the creative ideas of the students, generate many scenarios. I also work along with the groups to facilitate the planning, asking questions that help them organize their scenes. (An example is the following scene developed in my fifth grade: The players chose an old doll for their scene. The setting was in a bedroom of a young Jewish girl who was packing to leave for America during World War II. As the scene developed, it was revealed through the characters of the mother and grandmother that they were going to meet relatives in America. The young girl was told that she could take only one suitcase. She needed warm clothing and there was really no room for toys, but she could take one thing. She complains, but her parents are firm. When the scene ends, she has chosen the doll.)

Statues (a large group movement activity with an historical focus)

I introduce this activity with a discussion of statues, showing books, photos, or pictures of famous paintings or events that have created lasting images in history. I discuss the subject matter and the feelings conveyed. Once students understand the idea of the *statues* pantomime, they are ready to begin. (Note: Beforehand, I create a list of statue suggestions, which are drawn from familiar topics already introduced and researched in class.) All players, working individually, find a place to stand in the drama area. I tell them that as I play a rhythmic beat on my drum, they will walk in any direction around the drama area, and I caution them to work in their own space, not touching other players. When the drum stops, that is the signal to freeze. At this point, I call out a command, such as, "You are a member of the rock-throwing mob in the Boston Massacre." Each student strikes a pose and holds the statue in position. (Note: As the students gain confidence, the leader can ask a portion of the group to hold their statues while the others unfreeze and observe the statues. This process repeats until all sections have had the opportunity to show their statues.) Sample statue activities are as follows: The leader calls "freeze," and the students become

- a disguised Patriot throwing tea overboard on the ship *Beaver*
- a Native American seeing white settlers for the first time
- a pioneer clearing land to build a home
- a slave working in the cotton fields on the plantation
- a Civil War soldier behind a stone wall, waiting for the approaching enemy
- an immigrant seeing the Statue of Liberty for the first time from the deck of a ship
- a shirtwaist factory worker on strike in the picket line
- a civil rights activist on a protest march

Tableaux (a small group pantomime activity with an historical focus, which helps develop cooperation)

Historical fiction and nonfiction picture books are excellent resources for initiating this pantomime activity, named after the *tableaux vivants,* or living pictures, which began in European theatre of the Middle Ages. I select a book or a group of pictures to provide the idea for the tableaux. Together, we look at the pictures as I read the book or tell a story. Afterward, we list in sequential order the images or events that are depicted. Then, I divide the class into groups. Each group works to find a way to recreate one of the images. While groups are planning, I tell them to consider the feeling and the action they want to convey. I conference with each group during the planning stages. Groups perform each tableau in the sequence we listed. As students become more accomplished, each group can be responsible for entire tableaux, making a smooth transition from one image to another. (The following is a description, used in my fifth grade class, of a *Tableaux* activity prepared for a unit on slavery. I read to the class the picture book, *Now Let Me Fly*, by Dolores Johnson. We noted the excellent illustrations depicting the events in the story. We discussed the content, which reveals how Africans were forcibly taken from their homes and sold into slavery from the mid-1500s to the mid-1800s. I asked students to recall the major events in the book [for example, the brutal capture, the forced march to the coast, the agonizing voyage, the humiliating slave auction, the work in the cotton fields on the plantation]. Then I divided the class into five groups. Each group created tableaux that conveyed the events physically and emotionally. For example, one group might create three "living pictures" that depict the brutality of the capture: children clinging to mothers, some trying to flee, some cowering in fright, and so on.)

Variation of Tableaux (a large group movement activity)

This activity can be used as a follow-up to *Tableaux*. Instead of having groups in frozen poses (as in a tableau), groups plan a short movement piece connecting each tableau, making them come alive to communicate the idea through mime or movement. Acting as the facilitator, I conference with each group as they plan their movement. Each group then presents their movement piece. They take the tableau positions, come alive to show the movement sequence, then freeze while the next group performs. (An example of this drama activity is one experienced by my fifth graders and described here:

I used the same book, *Now Let Me Fly*, by Dolores Johnson. The students worked to communicate the ideas and feelings presented in the tableau piece but, this time, through movement. To help the students create visually interesting pieces, I suggested that they think about how to vary level, direction, tempo, and basic locomotor activities when preparing their movement. My role as a teacher–coach was crucial at this point in the activity. For students to create a mood that projected the emotion of the event, I used imagery. For this example, some of my coaching comments were: "Walk as if you had a large rock tied to your ankle." "Your space on the ship is so small, you feel as if you're locked in a trunk; there is little light or air." "Pick cotton as if you had just hiked for five hours in the August heat without any water.")

Why These Activities Are Important Preparation for More Challenging Drama/Theatre Projects

When I routinely use theatre games and creative drama activities, my students become comfortable participating in them. During the first few months of the school year, my goal is to have students develop the same comfort level they would have if playing a game during physical education, singing in music class, or painting in the art room. I start with the simple activities, such as pantomime. This allows the students to first express themselves with their bodies without having to worry about dialogue. After they have developed *confidence* with their bodies, the *cooperation* needed to create a tableau, for example, and the *concentration* that it takes to pass around an imaginary object or recall an emotion, then they are ready for more challenging scenes—those with dialogue. These scenes are called *improvisations*. They are scenes in which the actors create their dialogue as they go along.

The activities presented in this chapter are a sampling. They are those that I've used successfully with my classes over the years. There are other possibilities, however, and for a more extensive repertoire, I suggest using some of the books listed in this chapter's Resources. When I plan a social studies unit that relies on drama as a strategy, I go slowly through this preparation stage, trying many of these activities, choosing them with the needs of my group in mind. The time I spend on this is extremely important because it sets the stage for success with improvisational drama and involvement in theatre.

In the Spotlight: Two Lessons Using Pantomime

The In the Spotlight section is a detailed look at particular drama or social studies lessons. These lessons were originally used for an integrated social studies/ science unit focusing on environment, industrialization/technology, and cultural diversity. The historical understandings were the following:

- Native Americans and settlers had conflicting attitudes toward nature.
- The industrial revolution brought change and conflict.
- As citizens, we have a responsibility to value our natural resources.
- We can learn from past environmental mistakes.
- Community action groups have the power to enact change.

Lesson 1: Statues

1. To initiate the activity, I read the picture book, *A River Ran Wild*, by Lynne Cherry. It is the story of the Nashua River in New Hampshire and Massachusetts, settled by the Nashua Indian people. Soon English settlers came and with

them development and change. The growth of factories and towns along the banks of the river gradually polluted it until it was ecologically dead. Through community action, the river was eventually restored to its original state.

2. We discussed the themes of the book: the conflicting cultural viewpoints, the environment, the value of natural resources.

3. All students, working individually, participated in the drama activity called *Statues* (see this chapter for a description). In this activity, students find their own space in the drama area. When the teacher calls "freeze," the students create a pose of something depicted in the book. Examples of statues are a Nashua chief naming the river, a settler building a dam, a settler cutting down trees, deer drinking at the river, a pipe dumping pulp into the river, a citizen writing a letter to a politician, and Marion making speeches to organize the clean-up.

Lesson 2: Tableaux

1. Through discussion, we reviewed the major ideas of the book. We took another look at illustrations.

2. Students participated in the drama activity called *Tableaux* (see this chapter for a description). Working in groups of three or four, students created group tableaux based on scenes in the book. I directed the students to focus on conveying the idea both physically and emotionally. They planned how to make smooth transitions from one "living picture" to another.

The following are examples of the fifth grade tableaux:

Tableaux for group 1:

> Native people first seeing the Nashua River
> Natives trading fur
> Natives and settlers fighting

Tableaux for group 2:

> Settlers planting crops
> Factory workers lifting boxes in a paper mill
> Citizens protesting to politicians
> A 1990s family canoeing on the Nashua River

Ideas for Extension Activities

1. Students create improvisational dramas based on characters, settings, and conflicts in the book (see Chapter 3 for improvisation).

2. Students create improvisational dramas based on environmental problems

Figure 2–2. Students Participating in a Tableau

in their own community (an awareness of these problems would already have been developed during previous social studies/science lessons).

3. Students participate in a simulated town meeting or a debate on the issue of the river pollution and clean-up efforts (see Chapter 5 for these topics).

Evaluating the Student's Readiness for Learning Through Drama and Theatre

In this chapter, I emphasized the importance of having social skills in place before attempting any large-scale projects in drama and theatre. Being able to cooperate, concentrate, show respect to others, and participate thoughtfully in the problem-solving activities describes a student ready to assume a role in a creative drama or theatre activity. I spend the first few months of school observing my students carefully,

---

Student Self-Evaluation of Work in Social Studies/Drama Circle

	Always	Sometimes	Never

While participating in social studies/drama, I

1. listen respectfully to others

2. cooperate while working in group

3. share the responsibility for working
   on a group problem

4. participate in the discussions

5. work to find appropriate solutions
   to the problems the teacher presents

6. evaluate the work of others fairly

7. concentrate during the activity

8. make the best effort possible

Describe ways in which you have improved in social studies/drama since the start of the school year.

_____

What do you still need to do to improve your work in social studies/drama circle?

_____

Figure 2–3. Student Self-Evaluation of Work in Social Studies/Drama Circle

evaluating their work in drama circle, using an assessment checklist to document their behaviors (see Chapter 3). I also ask students to assess their participation in social studies/drama. The checklist in Figure 2–3 might help students focus on their self-evaluation.

Resources

Selected Professional Resources

D'Amboise, J. 1983. *Teaching the Magic of Dance*. New York: Simon and Schuster. D'Amboise, a professional dancer, gives an enthusiastic description of teaching dance in public elementary schools in New York City. In this inspiring book, he makes the case for using dance and movement as a medium for learning.

McCaslin, N. 1996. *Creative Drama in the Classroom and Beyond*, 6th ed. New York: Longman. This comprehensive book covers all facets of creative drama and theatre in education. Chapters 4, 5, and 6 focus on movement, pantomime, and improvisation. These chapters are filled with practical ideas that can be used in the elementary and middle grade classroom.

Spolin, V. 1986. *Theatre Games for the Classroom*. Chicago: Northwestern University Press. This is a book filled with theatre games (150+), listed sequentially from the simple to the challenging. Each game is presented in a recipe-like fashion so it can be read and understood with ease.

Walker, P. P. 1993. *Bring in the Arts*. Portsmouth, NH: Heinemann. The lesson plan format makes this book easy to follow. Part I includes lessons in movement, improvisation, and theatre games.

Wills, B. 1996. *Theatre Arts in the Elementary Classroom, Grades 4–6*. New Orleans: Anchorage Press. This comprehensive text is designed for classroom teachers with little or no experience using drama in the classroom. Each activity is listed by grade level and emphasizes the collaborative nature of theatre arts.

Zakkai, J. 1997. *Dance As a Way of Knowing*. York, ME: Stenhouse. Detailed model lessons take the teacher through warm-ups and movement explorations, showing the reader how to integrate these problem-solving activities into the curriculum.

A Sampling of Read-Alouds for Movement/Mime Activities

Bales, C.A. 1977. *Tales of the Elders: A Memory Book of the Men and Women Who Came to America As Immigrants, 1900–1930*. New York: Follett.

Cherry, L. 1992. *A River Ran Wild*. New York: Harcourt, Brace, Jovanovich.

Emert, P. R., ed. 1995. *Colonial Triangle Trade: An Economy Based on Human Misery*. Carlisle, MA: Discovery Enterprises, Ltd.

Johnson, D. 1993. *Now Let Me Fly*. New York: Alladin.

Leitner, I. 1993. *The Big Lie: A True Story*. New York: Scholastic.

Lyons, M. 1992. *Letters from a Slave Girl*. New York: Atheneum Books for Young Readers.

Marks, J. 1993. *The Hidden Children: The Secret Survivors of the Holocaust*. New York: Fawcett Columbine.

Meltzer, M. 1987. *The American Revolutionaries: A History in Their Own Words, 1750–1800*. New York: Crowell.

———. 1984. *The Black Americans: A History in Their Own Words*. New York: HarperCollins.

Paulsen, G. 1993. *Nightjohn*. New York: Delacorte.

Polacco, P. 1994. *Pink and Say*. New York: Philomel.

Yolen, J. 1992. *Encounter*. New York: Harcourt Brace.

3

Improvising and Recreating the Past

In a crowded meeting room, we intently watched a videotape of a group of students engaged in a dramatic improvisation in my fifth grade class. I was presenting a workshop at a social studies conference, sharing teaching strategies with the teachers there. I could tell, by observing their reaction, that they were impressed by the students' purposeful actions, sincere delivery, and the overall quality of the piece. A German soldier, searching a house for hidden Jews during World War II, spoke in a gruff voice: "Your neighbors, the Rosens, are missing. You will not object if we look around. We'll start in the bedroom." The scene continued, inspired by the book *Number the Stars,* as the students recreated the situation of fear brought on by Hitler's dictatorship. When the tape ended, a few teachers voiced their reactions: "They were really into it, so serious." "What did you do?" "No one was fooling around." I shared my ideas about why I thought it was successful, telling them that the improvisational activity had been carefully planned and organized. The scene had been derived through a developmental process, and this was the result. The kids were highly motivated because they were given the opportunity to create something while they were learning about history. By the end of this improvisation and related studies, the students had a clearer understanding of the persecution of Jews during World War II and of the underground resistance. They had become these people from the story, sharing the situation emotionally and physically. They were immersed in history, and enjoying it.

As the workshop session went on, other teachers shared with me their concern about using improvisational drama. They thought the idea of spontaneously creating scenes in the classroom was frightening, an unstructured risky situation. I told them that after using this strategy during many years of classroom practice in a variety of school settings, I had found that an improvisational drama lesson is no different from any other lesson. What is required of teachers is already a familiar everyday practice to them in a process-oriented classroom: Plan the lesson with clear objectives in mind, motivate the learners, act as facilitator to help learners plan and organize, pose questions for discussion and revision, and expect the best quality work.

Improvisational drama is, by definition, a scriptless type of drama. Students make up the dialogue as they go along. In the *Number the Stars* scene, students created the improvisation by using the literature as the basis for the plot idea. With me acting as the facilitator, it gradually developed into a clear dramatic piece. Other approaches to classroom drama, such as Dorothy Heathcote's "mantle of expert" approach (1995), suggest that the teacher "in role" assume a part alongside the students. For purposes of clarification, the Heathcote style of drama is not described in this chapter (although, at times, I do jump in a scene to play a role alongside the students for the purposes of modeling an idea or moving the scene along). What I do present is based on years of experience and experimentation, observing what works and what doesn't. The result, I feel, is a practical, workable approach for using dramatic improvisation as a teaching tool, especially in a social studies class where the historical content of the dramatic work is important. The improvisations outlined in this chapter may serve as a guide to teachers, including those with no formal background in drama, as to how creative drama might be used and structured in the social studies classroom.

The interaction of the teacher with students, as well as group cooperation, is crucial for successful explorations of history through drama, which is why I work hard to develop a cooperative and safe classroom atmosphere at the start of the year. If I've carefully set the stage for learning through drama, as suggested in Chapter 2, the children have already developed, to a degree, some confidence, cooperative learning techniques, and the concentration it takes to develop a scene. Then we move to new and more challenging experiences. Kids love participating in improvisation, but I've found that to make it a worthwhile experience, I need to set ground rules, plan the lesson carefully, treat it as a process, model the process, and incorporate research.

Setting the Ground Rules

Spending a lot of time working with the class on social skills at the outset of the year helps me when I start working on improvisational drama. Children then know that I expect them to listen carefully to me and others, respect the efforts of all students, cooperate, concentrate, and share the responsibility for working on a problem. They all know the word that signals "stop." In my class, I use the word *freeze*. Any word can be used as long as all the kids know that when they hear it, it means all action stops and there is an immediate silence. We usually practice this at the start of the year.

Planning the Lesson

Before the first drama session, I've already decided on the thematic content of the social studies unit (see detailed planning of a unit in Chapter 6). I've also read widely on the subject, collected materials for the children to use in the classroom, reserved books at the library, and located primary source documents and other resources, such as videotapes and musical recordings.

I usually prepare for an improvisational drama session by finding a good piece of literature on which we can base a scene. I've also used photos, invited speakers, and introduced newspaper articles and videotapes as resource material. Over the years, I've learned to recognize dramatic moments in history and in the lives of famous people. I look for conflict (the Patriots versus the British soldiers, the mill girls versus the mill owners). I try to find situations that can involve all the students (a classroom, meeting, courtroom, demonstration, mob, etc.). Once I've decided on the material, I use it to motivate the lesson and initiate a student discussion, followed by a scene-planning session.

As in Writing, Creative Drama Is a Process

Improvisational drama has many similarities to the process of writing. When I prepare a scene with the students, I take them through a series of steps: brainstorming, planning, the first playing (drafting), reflecting and revising, replaying. Exciting scenes, in most instances, don't happen on the first try; they evolve. Similarly, great writing doesn't take place with the first draft. In the drama process, students, working with me as facilitator, gradually build scenes that have interest and meaning. In some instances, they invent characters, settings, conflict, movement, voices, dialogue, and all the important details that communicate an idea to an audience. At other times, the characters, setting, and conflict already exist in literature, and students interpret how this scene would look if dramatized. My role as facilitator is an important one. Just as in a writing conference, my questions prompt the writer to make decisions about what to take out and what to develop, so too in an improvisational drama session, the questions posed by me help the students reflect and take steps to revise their work as they replay it in another session. I ask a lot of questions before, during, and after the improvisation.

Modeling Improvisational Drama Confirms That It Is a Process

Before students create group scenes on their own, I spend a number of weeks (sometimes months) working with the entire class on improvisational scenes, modeling the process: the motivation, the brainstorming and planning, playing the scene, the reflection and revision, replaying, and the final stage. The following steps, although not meant to be a "how-to" prescription for using improvisational drama, will provide some guidance as to how the process would look when applied to a learning situation in a social studies classroom.

The Motivation

To motivate and inspire the students in an historical drama activity, I try to choose a good "opener." I pick something that will spark the interest of the students, initiating their curiosity and generating a flow of questions. For example, in a social studies literature unit that focused on civil rights and Langston Hughes, I motivated the activity with a read-aloud session. The selection was chosen from an article in *The Langston Hughes Reader* (Hughes 1958) entitled, "My Most Humiliating Jim Crow Experience." Hughes vividly describes an incident in which a cashier in a cafeteria charged him an exorbitant price for food that he had selected, and not being able to afford the racially motivated price, he was forced to leave, embarrassed in front of his teen-age classmates. This selection was a workable choice for the following reasons:

1. The cafeteria setting was a familiar one to children, making it easier for them to improvise.
2. The dramatic situation allowed everyone to participate.
3. For students inexperienced with the process, there was a ready-made plot with a beginning, middle, climax, and end. This solved the problem of creating one. (Later, when the students are more comfortable with the process, I encourage them to create their own plots based on historical situations.)
4. It also contained conflict (central to any drama) and dramatic dialogue, which captured the interest of the listeners.
5. Finally, the dramatically written story generated many questions from the students when it was over: "Why did the cashier do that? What did the restaurant owner do? What did his friends say? When did this happen? Where did he live? Who is Jim Crow?" and so on. Through discussion, some of the questions were answered. Other questions were formulated and added to a list to be answered in study groups.

Brainstorming and Planning

During this stage, we create an outline for the improvisation. Working in the drama circle, the class gathers in front of the easel, and I record responses to questions on chart paper. The questions for the cafeteria scene might look something like this:

- Who are the characters in the scene?

- Where does the scene take place?
- How can we set up the acting space to look like a cafeteria?
- What is the main problem or conflict?
- What feelings motivated the cashier to behave that way?
- Did all the customers have similar feelings?
- How did Langston react?

This is much like the planning stage for a piece of fiction writing, during which I encourage students to create plot outlines and character descriptions. The results of a brainstorm session in preparation for the improvisation that we called "The White Tower Cafeteria" looked something like this:

Who:
    Langston Hughes
    Langston's best friend
    a cashier
    customers (classmates, strangers)
Where: a self-service cafeteria
What (conflict or problem): Langston wants to eat with his high school friend, but he can't afford the "special price" charged to him by the racially preju-diced cashier. He is forced to leave.

With this sketchy outline, we are ready to begin the drama session. Character choices are made, with me acting as the facilitator. I remind the actors that the scene will be repeated during several sessions and that they will have the opportunity to rotate in the major speaking roles. We decide where actors will be at the start of the scene and how the stage area should be set up. In this case, we lined up a few desks to represent a cafeteria-style serving area, set a chair and another desk for the cashier, and scat-tered chairs in small groupings around the acting space to represent customer tables.

At this point, I expect the students to move desks quickly (if necessary), set up the drama area for the scene, gather a few props, and take their places either on or off the "stage" area, as we agreed in the planning.

Playing the Scene

Before the "curtain," I instruct students that while playing the scene, they are to listen to my voice, respond to it, but continue the action of the scene without com-ing out of character. My interjections or questions are referred to as "side coach-ing." It helps the student actors think about how to communicate their ideas clearly to the "audience" (the teacher). Throughout an improvisation, students are solving problems—individual and group problems. The side coaching keeps them actively thinking about ways to show the audience their character, and to clearly reveal the character's relationships to other characters. The following are typical side-coaching questions or comments for the cafeteria scene:

- How can you show, through your body, what you are feeling?
- How can you show that he is your best friend?
- Make the food real. How do you feel about what you are eating?
- How can you show your anger?
- Cashier, how can you show that you are stubborn and filled with hatred?
- Customers, how do you react? Are you surprised? Shocked? Do you agree with the cashier? Do you feel sorry for Langston? Are you confused by the commotion?

While playing the scene, students need to listen to each other, concentrate on revealing the scenario, and work to develop their character. I also remind them to keep action to a minimum and dialogue in pantomime when the main characters are speaking.

Reflection and Revision

The first time a scene is improvised, it finishes quickly as students choose only the essential plot elements to convey the drama. Much like the first draft of a story, it's sketchy and lacks detail. Characters are exaggerated and sometimes stereotypical. (The cashier, for example, might be portrayed as a snarling, mean old woman.)

When it is time for the students to begin the process of reflection, they sit again in the drama circle, and I assume the role of the facilitator. Similar to a writer's conference, I ask questions and listen carefully. A sampling of my questions might look something like these:

- Which parts were the most exciting?
- Which parts didn't work and were not needed?
- Which parts were the most believable?
- How can we make the action more believable?
- Was the conflict clear to the audience?
- How can we establish the setting more clearly for the audience?
- What does the audience need to know in this part of the scene?
- How can we reveal the relationship between the two characters?
- What dialogue can these characters develop?

As the student responses are made, we discuss them, agreeing or disagreeing. I voice my opinion and suggestions from the audience's point of view. I record on chart paper a list of suggestions for revisions to be posted and used as a reminder for the next drama session.

Replaying the Scene

When playing the scene a second time, the conflict becomes clearer to the "audience." The additional actions and dialogue create more dramatic interest and help reveal the characters and setting. I continue the side coaching as a way of reinforcing what works and encouraging all to be thinking critically as they work through the scene. Revision continues with a focus on character development. One way I encourage this is to have students create a biographical sketch for their character. Following is a sampling of questions that I might ask them to consider when preparing a character sketch for this scene:

- How old is your character?
- What does your character do for a living?
- What food does your character select from the cafeteria?
- How is your character feeling today? Are you physically comfortable?
- What does your character feel toward Langston?
- Is your character involved or disinterested in this situation?
- How does your character move?
- Is your character quiet or talkative?
- How does your character speak?
- What type of clothing would your character be wearing?

These questions and others are designed to promote subtle actions in the characters as they interact with each other during the improvisation. Through these actions, the characters are gradually revealed to the audience.

At this point in scene development, I ask questions related to the setting and how the setting influences the character's actions. Examples of these questions might be the following:

- How can you show that you're too hot while standing in line, wearing a winter coat?
- How can you show the audience that there is a wide array of food along the cafeteria counter?
- Would you eat differently in a cafeteria than you would in your own house?
- Does the sight of all the food make you hungry?

In subsequent sessions, the revisions continue as I encourage my students to solve the problems presented during reflective discussion. Each time a scene is repeated, more details are added, dialogue is refined, and a sense of rhythm emerges.

The Final Stage of the Process

I don't always take a scene to this level, especially when students are just beginning to explore the use of improvisational drama. I find that repeating it two or

Figure 3–1. Improvisational Drama Brought to Performance Level. RIC Office of News & Public Relations, Gordon Rowley, Photographer

three times is enough at the start. The students benefit from the discussions, the historical content, and the problem-solving practice. Time is also a factor. Taking them through the process is time consuming, and I don't always have the time to spend perfecting a scene. However, there are occasions when you might want to share scenes with an audience, incorporating them into a scripted performance. If this is the case, then it is important to have clarity in the plot development, dialogue, characterizations, and line delivery.

In the final stage of scene development, the details that help create a mood become the focus. I encourage student actors to be aware of their voices and how they deliver a line. I ask them to think about what motivates their characters' behavior. Students, at this stage, add more props and choose a costume piece to suggest their character. Stacked crates, stocked with a variety of hats, shawls, aprons, vests, scarves, purses, briefcases, and a wide variety of hand props are available for choosing. Helping to create a mood, the costume pieces and props also change the young student actors, giving them more confidence and infusing the scene with excitement.

The process of scene development seems rather long, but the students are engaged at all times solving the problems presented before each session, and I've never observed that the learners appeared bored during drama. When possible, I try to schedule social studies/drama sessions along with independent or guided research. As children learn new information about the topic, they bring that knowledge to the drama session and the reflective discussions.

Balancing Drama Activities with Literature and Research

When I start with a memorable read-aloud and improvisation, like the one previously described, I find that the students are motivated to want more information on the subject. They want to know what caused the situation. In fact, they are asking for the context in which this event occurred. In the example of Langston Hughes' humiliating Jim Crow experience, there were many subjects that needed to be considered for my kids to truly understand why this happened when it did. Jim Crow laws, the African American's long fight for civil rights, the migration of Southern blacks to the North during and after World War I, and the post-war as a time of rapid change in society and technology were all subjects that were important to an understanding of the context.

In addition to the dramatic improvisations, students participated in a variety of activities in conjunction with this same topic: listening to read-alouds, viewing documentary videotape, reading and discussing the poetry of Hughes, writing poetry, and writing responses to poetry, historical fiction, and the improvisational experiences.

Students were also responsible for research and reading individually or in small groups. In this instance, I required each student to read a biography on Langston Hughes and one historical fiction from a list of three for literature group discussion. In addition, they had to prepare an in-depth research project on a narrower topic of their choice. Small groups or individuals then became "experts" on a particular subject. This knowledge, in some instances, was applied to the creation of a whole class play project on the life of Langston Hughes.

Where to Find Ideas for Improvisations

I find ideas for historical improvisations from dramatic events in history and in the lives of famous and ordinary people. When planning a social studies unit, I first consider the concepts to be taught. With the concepts in mind, I then choose a dramatic account of an event, an excerpt from an autobiography or biography, a primary document such as a letter or diary, to provide the inspiration and basic core of ideas for an improvisational scene. For instance, I used the autobiography of Frederick Douglass and the diary of the slave Solomon Northup as a framework for students to develop historical understandings about slavery and pre–Civil War history. I rely heavily on literature, both fiction and nonfiction, for ideas, and I choose material that has a potential for conflict, because conflicting ideas or characters are the basis from which a dramatic situation grows into a scene.

The historical improvisations that follow are examples of ideas tried in my class, with students working as an ensemble or in small groups. All of the topics focus on American history, part of the fifth grade curriculum. These scenarios are outlined in detail to provide structure for teachers who would like to experiment with improvisational drama in their social studies classes.

Improvisation 1: The Boston Massacre and the Aftermath (1770)

> Counsel ought to be the very last thing that an accused person should (lack) in a free country. The bar ought in my opinion to be independent and impartial at all times and in every circumstance. Persons whose lives are at stake ought to have the counsel they prefer.
>
> John Adams (referring to his taking on the defense of Captain Preston in the Boston Massacre Trial)

Source of Inspirational Material

The Story of the Boston Massacre, by Mary Kay Phelan

Historical Understanding

The political effects of the Boston Massacre were far-reaching. The event, sometimes referred to as the first battle of the American Revolution, strengthened the colonists' resistance toward Great Britain.

Ideas Revealed Through the Source Material

- The confrontation on March 5th between British soldiers and Boston citizens was the result of months of tension build-up.
- The Boston mob taunted the soldiers, threw sticks, knocked soldiers down, and dared the British soldiers to fire their guns. British soldiers, in a panic, fired into the crowd.
- Captain Preston and eight men were arrested.
- Preston was defended by John Adams.
- Patriots, although eager to prove that there should be justice for all men, were annoyed at John Adams for taking the case.

Scene 1 Outline: The Arrest

Who: Governor Hutchinson, Captain Preston, an angry mob of townspeople, British soldiers, Justices Richard Dana and John Tudor

Where: The Town House (midnight of March 5, 1770)

What (scenario as developed in the improvisational sessions): The scene opens with cries of angry townspeople pouring into the council chamber of the Town House. Governor Hutchinson tries to quiet the crowd, expressing concern that more violence can only lead to a worse catastrophe. He promises that if the Captain and the soldiers are found guilty, they will be brought to justice and punished according to the law. Justices Richard Dana and John Tudor arrive, and the interrogation of Captain Preston and the eight soldiers begins. The justices listen to the testimony of witnesses and question Preston and the soldiers. They recount their version of the evening's events. After consideration, the judges decide that there is sufficient evidence to imprison Captain Preston and the eight soldiers. The citizens react with wild joy.

Scene 2 Outline: The New Client

Who: John Adams, James Forrest (a prosperous merchant)

Where: The law office of John Adams (early morning, the next day)

What: John Adams is working at his desk when there is a frantic pounding on the door. He tells the person to enter, and a man (Forrest) rushes in, behaving hysterically. He tells Adams about the jailing of Captain Preston and says that he brings a personal request from Preston, who wishes John Adams to be his lawyer. Forrest explains that he has already tried three lawyers for the Crown, but they have all refused to take the case, fearing the wrath of the Patriots. Adams believes that everyone has the right to representation, so he agrees to take the case. Adams continues, telling Forrest that his new client can expect "nothing more than fact, evidence, and the law will justify."

Scene 3 Outline: Who Buys Lobsters?

Who: An angry mob, Abigail Adams, John Adams

Where: The house of John Adams

What: An angry mob is chanting outside John Adams' house: "Who buys lobsters? Who buys lobsters?" As the lawyer passes through the crowd to enter his house, there are whistles, catcalls, and mud thrown at him. He enters the house, and the crowd disperses. Abigail rushes to greet him, concerned for his safety. Adams sees a window broken and two bricks on the floor. Abigail explains that, moments earlier, the crowd threw the bricks through the window. He inquires about the safety of the children. She reassures him that they are fine, but she is seriously worried that his life is in danger. John emphasizes that there is no need for anxiety. It has been months since the massacre, and tempers have cooled. Citizens are more reasonable now and they are willing to let justice prevail.

Linking the Past to the Present

Question to consider: In what ways could the Boston Massacre be compared with the violent attack on youths in Tiananmen Square?

Improvisation 2: Willy Freeman Testifies in Court

. . . the next thing I knew there was British soldiers all around him (Pa) and I saw a bayonet go through his back and he flung his arms out like so, and fell off the bayonet to the ground. I began to shriek. The shouting and killing went on and on, and I crouched on the platform with my eyes closed, crying and moaning and waiting to be killed.

Willy Freeman (an eyewitness account of the massacre at Fort Griswold)

Source of Inspirational Material

War Comes to Willy Freeman, by J.L. Collier & C. Collier (Note: Willy Freeman is a fictional character who interacts with real people and real events in the Collier & Collier book.)

Historical Understanding

During the American Revolution, slavery was legal in both the North and the South.

Ideas Revealed Through the Source Material

- Slaves who fought in the American Revolution were given their freedom.
- Some slaves fought as a substitute for their masters who didn't want to fight.
- Masters were given a bounty as compensation for freeing a slave, who was their property, to fight in the war.

Scene Outline: The Trial of Jack Arabus Versus Captain Ivers

Who: The Judge (James Wadsworth), Captain Ivers, Mr. Chauncy (Ivers' lawyer), Willy Freeman, Mr. Goodrich (Arabus' Lawyer), Jack Arabus, courtroom spectators

Where: a New Haven courtroom

What (the scenario, as developed in improvisational sessions, was based mostly on the historical fiction book): As the scene begins, Mr. Chauncy is assuring

Captain Ivers that he has nothing to worry about. The law, he says, is on the side of white Christian gentlemen, not in favor of black slaves. Captain Ivers brags that he'll have his slave (Arabus) back by the end of the day. Willy and Mr. Goodrich arrive. This amuses Captain Ivers, who jokes that she'll get her punishment for assaulting him. Judge Wadsworth comes in, and the session begins. Mr. Chauncy presents a bill of sale for Jack Arabus, showing that he purchased Jack. Mr. Goodrich, in turn, presents papers that prove Captain Ivers manumitted Jack Arabus when Arabus went as a substitute soldier for Captain Ivers. He points out that Ivers received an allowance compensating him for the loss of a slave. Mr. Chauncy has no argument against these facts, but he says that his client was assaulted by Willy Freeman. Mr. Goodrich, in return, charges Captain Ivers with assaulting Willy. The judge calls Willy to testify. She tells the entire story of her mother's death due to Ivers' neglect. She also reveals that she is, by law, entitled to be free because her father fought and died in the war. The lawyers continue to argue, but in the end, the judge decides that both Jack Arabus and Willy are free citizens. Captain Ivers, in frustration and anger, yells at the judge and stalks out of the courtroom.

Improvisation 3: In the Slave Quarters with Frederick Douglass

The songs of the slaves represent the sorrows of his heart, and he is relieved by them only as an aching heart is relieved by its tears.

Frederick Douglass

Source of Inspirational Material

Narrative of the Life of Frederick Douglass, by Frederick Douglass (Chapters 2 and 5)
The Story of Frederick Douglass, by Eric Weiner
Frederick Douglass, Voice of Liberty, by Melissa Banta

Historical Understanding

Slaves were denied basic human rights.

Ideas Revealed Through the Source Material

- Living conditions on the plantation were degrading.
- Slaves sang to express sorrow or longing.
- Slave owners often used violent, cruel, and inhuman treatment to control slaves.
- It was unlawful to teach a slave how to read and write.

Scene Outline: In the Slave Quarters

Who: Frederick Douglass, slaves, the overseer, the Master
Where: a slave cabin on the plantation
What (the scenario as developed during improvisational sessions): It is late at night and the slaves are singing a forbidden song, "Go Down Moses." There is a discussion about two slaves who have made a run for it that night. Frederick is drawing letters on the dirt floor, and he is warned by an elder about the danger of getting caught knowing how to read and write. Frederick contends that he is not afraid of the overseer. All go to sleep on the dirt floor. In the morning, the food arrives in a trough. Slaves eat the mush with their hands or oyster shells. The overseer arrives with a large hickory stick in hand, followed by the Master. They question the slaves about the runaways. The Master promises freedom to the one who gives information. He walks around, looking at each slave. There is a tense silence. The Master then notices the writing in the dirt and asks who wrote it. Frederick, not wanting anyone else to get punished, admitted he did it, telling the Master that he was only imitating the shapes that were on the side of the crates that he was hauling yesterday. The Master reminds Frederick that it is illegal for slaves to write, and as an example, he will be punished with the whip. The overseer grabs Frederick and hauls him offstage.

Linking the Past to the Present

Question to consider: In what countries of the world is slavery still practiced?

Improvisation 4: The Mill Girls Organize to Fight Poor Labor Conditions

Our heart, yea our whole soul, is wrapped up in the cause of the oppressed, of the downtrodden millions throughout the world.

Sarah G. Bagley (*Voice of Industry*, 1845)

Source of Inspirational Material

The Mill Girls, by Bernice Selden (Book Three, Chapters 1, 2, 3)
Lyddie, by Katherine Paterson

Historical Understanding

Owners of textile mills took advantage of a labor force that was not organized and was composed largely of women.

Ideas Revealed Through the Source Material

- Mill hours were long (13 to 14 hours each day).
- Mills were dirty, polluted with cotton fiber, hot in summer, cold in winter. The noise of the machines was deafening.
- Workers were subject to lung disease.
- Overseers were cruel, pushing operatives to work faster.
- Attempts were made by women to organize labor against unfair practices.
- Sarah G. Bagley organized the Female Labor Reform Association.
- Workers were threatened with dismissal if they joined a labor organization or signed a petition.
- Those who staged a "turnout" (a walkout) were fired and blacklisted from working in any other mills.
- In 1845, the Massachusetts legislature appointed a special House Committee to investigate labor conditions in the mills.

Beginning the Improvisation

The ideas for the two improvisational scenes that follow were generated from the question, "What if Lyddie Worthen and Sarah G. Bagley were friends working in the same mill?"

Scene 1 Outline: The Turnout

Who: Lyddie Worthen, Sarah G. Bagley, the overseer, mill workers
Where: Meeting of the Female Labor Reform Association
  The Mill (early morning)
  The Mill (later that day)
What (the scenario as developed during improvisational sessions): At a meeting of the Female Labor Reform Association, Sarah reads a petition that she will send to the Massachusetts legislature in support of a ten-hour work day and better conditions at the mill. Most agree to sign the petition. Sarah encourages workers to stage a turnout (a walkout) as a protest against the long hours. She argues that the overseer will agree to anything to keep the machines running and the owner happy. Most workers pledge to go along with the turnout, signing their names to the petition. Lyddie does not sign the pledge.

  At the starting bell the next morning, workers file in past the overseer, Lyddie is called into his office. He questions her about the association meeting and offers her a full week's wages if she names all those workers who have signed the petition or belong to the association. Lyddie gives no information. Later that day, at the afternoon starting bell, only a dozen workers walk off

46

the job. The workers, including Lyddie, are fired immediately by the overseer and given a dishonorable discharge, which blacklists them from working in any other mill.

Scene 2 Outline: The Hearing to Investigate Labor Conditions

Who: Members of the investigating committee, a variety of mill operatives (both men and women), Sarah G. Bagley, Chairman of the Committee

Where: A committee meeting room at the Massachusetts State House

What (the scenario as developed during improvisational sessions): The Chairman convenes the session, stating its purpose. One by one, the mill operatives are called in front of the House committee. They are questioned about working conditions, hours, and pay. Each worker testifies, telling the story of their mill. (Note: Based on their research, students can prepare their testimony ahead of time.)

Linking the Past to the Present

Questions to consider: What protections do workers have against unfair labor practices today? How are factory workers treated in Third World countries?

Improvisation 5: Trouble Erupts at School over the Issue of Slavery (1851)

On this subject (slavery), I do not wish to think, or speak, or write with moderation. No! No! Tell a man whose house is on fire, to give a moderate alarm, . . . tell the mother to gradually extricate her babe from the fire into which it has fallen, . . . but urge me not to use moderation in a course like the present.

William Lloyd Garrison (from "Manifesto," *The Liberator,* Jan. 1, 1831)

Source of Inspirational Material

"'For the Sake of Commerce': Rhode Island, Slavery, and the Textile Industry," an essay by Myron O. Stachiw

History You Can See: Scenes of Change in Rhode Island, 1790–1910, by H. Davis and N. Robinson

Historical Understandings

- Abolitionists, people opposed to slavery, formed antislavery groups.
- The issue of slavery caused conflict among Northerners.
- Many Northern merchants and manufacturers were dependent on the system of slavery for their economic success.

Ideas Revealed Through the Source Material

- The issue of slavery divided Northerners, often the wealthy against the middle class.
- Abolitionists and antiabolitionist groups were active in Rhode Island.
- Rhode Island mill owners bought cotton from Southern planters to manufacture "Negro cloth" (a generic name for a coarse material produced exclusively for slaves),which was then sold back to the slave owners.
- In 1850, seventy percent of the cloth manufactured in Rhode Island mills was "Negro cloth."

Scene Outline: The Trouble at School

Who: the teacher, students of all ages, son of a local mill owner, a boy who is a Quaker, the teacher's friend

Where: a one-room schoolhouse in Rhode Island, 1851

What (the scenario as developed during improvisational sessions): The students are practicing a patriotic song. After the music, the teacher conducts a history lesson on the triangle slave trade in Rhode Island. Students ask questions about slavery because it is a topic that everyone is talking about at home and in the newspapers. Students voice opinions, imitating ideas heard from their parents. A few make derogatory remarks about the local mill owner who does business with Southern planters, making big profits selling "Negro cloth." The students argue about whether or not it is evil to make and sell cloth for the sole purpose of clothing slaves. The son of the mill owner defends his father's actions. The Quaker boy refers to the mill owner as a greedy, evil man. The mill owner's son hits him and a fist fight erupts. The teacher stops the fight, threatening both with dismissal from school. The teacher's friend arrives at this point and helps to calm the class. When the students settle into working, the friend takes the teacher aside to tell her that Frederick Douglass is speaking that evening at an antislavery meeting. They agree to go together. (Note: Through research, the students found that a patriotic song that was written in the 1840s was "Columbia the Gem of the Ocean," sometimes known as "Red, White and Blue.")

Linking the Past to the Present

Questions to consider: Are there issues that passionately divide citizens today? What issues cause corporations and environmentalists to be at odds with each other? What organized groups exhibit racism today?

Extension Activity

Performance of a full-length play, *The Loom and the Lash,* which is about a family's conflict during the time of Southern slavery and Northern industrialization.

Improvisation 6: The Orphans Are "Placed Out"

> Most touching of all was the crowd of wandering little ones who immediately found their way to the office . . . all this motley throng of infantile misery and childhood guilt passed through our doors, telling their simple stories of suffering and loneliness, and temptation, until our hearts became sick.
>
> Rev. Charles Loring Brace, 1853 (in reference to the opening of the Children's Aid Society)

Source of Inspirational Material

> *The Orphan Trains: Leaving the Cities Behind,* edited by Jeanne Munn Bracken (pp. 5–19)
> *Orphan Train Rider: One Boy's True Story,* by Andrea Warren (Chapters 2 and 3)
> *A Family Apart,* by Joan Lowery Nixon (Chapters 4 and 5)

Historical Understanding

The Industrial Revolution brought growth to cities, and with growth came social problems. There were no welfare programs to support families if the wage earners were sick or disabled, or had died.

Ideas Revealed Through the Source Material

- There was no welfare system in the 1800s.
- Children were forced out of their homes by desperate parents, and they had to survive in the streets, stealing to eat.
- In 1850, there were an estimated 30,000 homeless children roaming the streets of New York City.
- Rev. Charles Loring Brace founded the Children's Aid Society in 1853.
- Beginning in 1854, trains carried orphans to the midwest and other parts of the United States to be "placed out" with families.

Scene Outline: Ragamuffins Come to the Children's Aid Society

> *Who:* Charles Loring Brace, homeless children, a charitable woman, an agent for the society, the Kelly children (Frances, Mike, Petey, Danny, Meghan, Peg), trip attendant

Where: the office of the Children's Aid Society

What (the scenario as developed during improvisational sessions): The Children's Aid Society is crowded and noisy. There is a woman at a desk (agency worker) and a long line of children in front of her. As each child steps up, they are questioned by the agency worker and she records the information. Each child has a sad story to tell about their homeless situation. Charles Loring Brace arrives with the six Kelly children. He settles them on a bench to wait their turn, gives them a little information about what will happen next, and leaves. A woman arrives with a donation of clothing for the homeless children. Frances Kelly overhears the agency worker say that boys are more easily placed in homes than are girls because boys can do farm chores. She tells her sisters and brothers of her plan. She grabs some old clothes, goes out into an alley and returns shortly dressed as a boy. When it is their turn with the agency worker, Frances passes for a boy. Later, the trip attendant arrives and explains the details of the train trip to the children. She describes how the train will stop at different stations in Missouri and that families will choose children to come live with them. The Kelly children express concern that they will be separated from each other. Petey is hysterical, calling for his Ma. Suddenly, the agency worker calls for quiet, lines the children up, and they all leave the society headed for the train station.

Linking the Past to the Present

Question to consider: What programs and agencies help the poor, homeless, and unemployed today?

Improvisation 7: Langston Hughes Experiences Jim Crowism (circa 1917)

Our high school class had gone to see a performance of Sarah Bernhardt. . . . The magic of her voice still rings in my ears. But of that afternoon, there is even a more vivid memory.

Langston Hughes (referring to his Jim Crow experience)

Source of Inspirational Material

"My Most Humiliating Jim Crow Experience," an article from *The Langston Hughes Reader,* by Langston Hughes

"Merry Go Round," from *The Dreamkeeper and Other Poems,* by Langston Hughes

Historical Understanding

Jim Crow laws segregated blacks from whites in most social, educational, and work situations.

Ideas Revealed Through the Source Material

- Jim Crow laws separated blacks from whites in restaurants, at lunch counters, at drinking fountains, in sports, and so on.
- Jim Crowism was discriminating and humiliating for black Americans, and denied them their civil rights.
- During World War I, large numbers of blacks migrated to the North in search of better jobs, better schools, and a chance to get ahead.

Scene Outline: *The White Tower Cafeteria*

Who: Langston Hughes, Langston's best friend, a cashier, customers, classmates

Where: a self-service cafeteria (Cleveland, Ohio, 1917)

What (the scenario as developed during improvisational sessions): Langston and a group of high school students enter the cafeteria. His classmates go through the line first, selecting their food and then paying the cashier. Langston and his friend are discussing the matinee performance of Sarah Bernhardt that they attended. His friend selects his food, pays for it, and moves on to find a table. Langston steps up to the cashier, and she starts ringing up the bill, pounding the keys, until the amount on the register tape grows larger and larger. Finally, she pulls out the tape and flings it at Langston, demanding the ridiculous total shown. Langston looks at the amount in amazement. He questions the cashier and an argument ensues. The cashier becomes more and more belligerent, until everyone in the cafeteria is listening to the argument and the line is growing behind Langston. Finally, she demands that he pay or get out. Langston puts down his tray and goes to his friend. It takes a long time to explain the situation to the astonished boy. He is indignant and wants to defend Langston, protest to the manager, or buy food for him. Langston, now embarrassed by all the commotion, decides to leave. His friend follows.

Linking the Past to the Present

Questions to consider: How did blacks protest Jim Crow laws in the 1950s and 1960s? What laws were passed in the 1960s that guaranteed civil rights to African Americans?

Improvisation 8: Underground Resistance in World War II

Their stories (those of Gentiles who helped rescue Jews) let us know that while there were victims, there were also heroes and heroines. What they did makes us see that we need not give in to evil. There are other choices than passive acceptance, or complicity. There are human spirits who resist. They are witness to the goodness of humanity.

Milton Meltzer (from *Rescue: The Story of How Gentiles Saved Jews in the Holocaust*)

Source of Inspirational Material

The three historical fiction books for the following scenes are

Scene I: *Number the Stars,* by Lois Lowry
Scene 2: *Snow Treasure,* by Marie McSwigan
Scene 3: *The Upstairs Room,* by Johanna Reiss

Historical Understanding

The underground resistance in German-occupied countries undermined German operations and helped some Jews escape to safety or hide until the war ended.

Ideas Revealed Through the Source Material

- During occupation, Nazis controlled the government, newspapers, the rail system, schools, hospitals, and the day-to-day operations of a country.
- Working for the Resistance or helping Jews to hide or escape was dangerous. If caught, the punishment was death.

Scene 1 Outline: And This Is My Sister Lise

Who: Annemarie Johansen, Mr. and Mrs. Johansen, Ellen Rosen, the Nazi soldiers
Where: The apartment of the Johansen's in Copenhagen, Denmark (1943)
What (the scenario as created from situations and characters presented in the book, *Number the Stars,* and developed during improvisational sessions): Annemarie and Ellen (a Jew being hidden by the Johansen's) are having dinner. Annemarie is describing to her parents how she was stopped by Nazi soldiers in the street and poked with a rifle. Mr. Johansen shares the news that Nazi soldiers are conducting house-to-house searches for hidden Jews. He reminds Ellen that she must pretend to be his daughter. Ellen and Annemarie prepare to go to bed. Nazis arrive and question Mr. and Mrs. Johansen as to where the Rosen family (who live downstairs) has disappeared. They search the apartment and go to the bedroom where Annemarie and Ellen are in bed.

The girls hear the Nazis approaching, and Annemarie tears the Star of David necklace off of Ellen's neck. The soldiers burst into the bedroom and pull the terrified girls out of bed to question them. The Nazis are suspicious because the girls do not resemble each other. Mr. Johansen pulls out a family photo album and shows pictures of the girls when they were babies. The Nazi soldiers make insulting remarks to Mrs. Johansen. After examining the photos, the soldier tears them up and throws them on the floor, grinding his heels into the pictures. He then leaves, followed by the two other soldiers. Everyone is relieved that the deception worked.

Scene 2 Outline: The Defense Club Meeting

Who: Peter Lundstrom, members of the defense club, three Nazi soldiers

Where: a house in Riswyk, Norway (1940)

What (the scenario as created from characters presented in the book, *Snow Treasure,* and developed during improvisational sessions): Peter is having a secret meeting of the Defense Club at his house. Two boys strongly object to having Peter lead the gold-smuggling operation. An argument among the children unfolds. Suddenly, they are interrupted by a pounding at the door. Nazi soldiers who have been patrolling the neighborhood have detected radio signals coming from Peter's house. The soldiers search the house for a wireless phone. Peter manages to get rid of the Nazis and handles the situation so well that the dissenting boys are convinced that Peter should be the leader of the smuggling operation. The scene ends with Peter organizing the first group to transport the gold on their sleds.

Scene 3 Outline: Nazis Search for Hidden Jews

Who: Sini, Annie, Mr. and Mrs. Oosterveld, Granny, two Nazi soldiers

Where: House of the Oostervelds in Holland (1943)

What (the scenario as created from situations and characters presented in the book, *Upstairs Room,* and developed during improvisational sessions): Annie (a young Jewish girl in hiding) is in the kitchen reading out loud and talking to Mrs. Oosterveld and Granny. Mr. Oosterveld returns home to announce that the Nazis are in the neighborhood, conducting a house-to-house search. They quickly hide Annie in her secret place in the closet. Before long, the soldiers arrive and conduct a search. While they are searching, Sini (the sister of Annie who is also in hiding) arrives unaware that the house is being searched. The Nazi soldiers, suspicious of her, demand that she show her papers. The Oostervelds, thinking quickly, say that Sini is their new maid. Mrs. Oosterveld then orders her to make tea and begin her work. The Oostervelds, pretending to be sympathetic to the Nazi cause, invite the soldiers to stay for tea and homemade biscuits. They agree, and sit to engage in a little small talk with the Oostervelds. Satisfied with the search, the soldiers leave. The Oostervelds take Annie out of hiding, and they all breathe a sigh of relief.

Linking the Past to the Present

Questions to consider: What countries are ruled by dictatorships today? What countries today, under the guise of nationalism, have slaughtered ethnic groups for their religious or political beliefs? Is it possible for another Holocaust to occur?

In the Spotlight: The Immigrant Experience

The first year that I included an immigration unit in my curriculum, I was inspired by a photography exhibit at the New York Historical Society. I saw a memorable collection of photographs by Jacob Riis and Lewis Hine, showing children working in factories, sleeping in the streets, or living in dark, filthy, one-room apartments in New York City. Many of these photographs, which appear in Russell Freedman's book, *Immigrant Kids*, proved to be useful as a springboard for discussion and scene ideas. Faced with the enormity of this topic (from the first boatload of settlers until now), I decided to focus on the period of highest immigration (early 1900s), and to make it a meaningful experience, connect it to present-day immigration in our state (Rhode Island). I felt that the attitudes that existed toward immigrants a hundred years ago were still prevalent today. By sharing a variety of literature as well as other resources, including firsthand accounts, students were able to create scenes that conveyed some of the hardships, discrimination, and racial stereotyping that immigrants encounter. As the students listened to or read these immigrant stories, I asked them to focus on the following questions:

- Why did this person (or family) immigrate to America?
- What were the greatest difficulties experienced when first arriving in a new country?
- What job opportunities existed for them?
- What type of discrimination did they endure?
- What types of living conditions did they encounter?
- What did the immigrants miss about the country they left behind?
- What expectations did they have for life in America?
- How is racial stereotyping evident in these stories?

After laying the foundation through reading, discussion, and research, we were ready to begin our improvisation. The following *In the Spotlight* drama activity describes how an improvisation developed to performance level, taking the reader through the various stages that I've described in this chapter: brainstorming and planning, playing the scene, reflection and revision, replaying the scene, and the final stage.

The Bullies at P.S. No. 1

> There was a bunch of young fellows there (on the stairs) talking to each other and having a lot of fun. I was their age, but I couldn't speak any English. I didn't want to step on their clothes, so I was kind of careful, and they realized that . . . so, he (one fellow) came to me and talked, 'blah, blah'. The first thing I know he gives me one upper cut and down I went. . . . Right then and there I made up my mind I'm going to school nights, learn the language, read, write, and spoken, and go to the YMCA to prepare myself to defend myself.
>
> Nicholas Gerros, a Greek immigrant remembering his youth (from *Coming to America: A New Life in a New Land*)

Source of Inspirational Material

Immigrant Kids, by Russell Freedman
Coming to America: A New Life in a New Land, edited by Katherine Emsden
Tales of the Elders: A Memory Book of Men and Women Who Came to America As Immigrants, 1900–1930, edited by C.A. Bales

Historical Understanding

Recent immigrants experience discrimination in a variety of ways. They have difficulties adjusting to a new culture and way of life.

Ideas Revealed Through the Source Material

- Immigrant children had difficulty in school because they couldn't speak English.
- Non–English-speaking immigrants were placed in classes with children much younger than they until they learned English.
- Recitation was a common method of learning.
- Schools had few frills and no special subjects.
- Many immigrant kids dropped out of school to work. At the turn of the century, it was an accomplishment just to finish grammar school.

Brainstorming and Planning

After sharing the Freedman book in the motivational activity, the brainstorm session began with the question, "What ideas from this book can we develop into a scene?"

There were lots of suggestions that involved gang fights, street games, crowded tenement living, but finally there was a consensus. The scene would take place in a classroom. My questions continued: "Who can be in the scene; everyone needs a part?" Kids and a teacher was the general response. "Who are these kids? Are they rich or poor? Are they immigrants? How do they behave in class?" Gradually, a variety of characters emerged: immigrants who can't speak English well, immigrants who have been in America for awhile, class bullies, a tattletale, a teacher's pet, the teacher, a principal, and so forth. The questioning went on: "What problem can we create to provide conflict for the drama?" It was agreed that, in this scene, the American students did not like the immigrant kids in the class. The immigrant kids were often dirty and strange in the way they talked, acted, and dressed. The bullies teased the immigrant kids, laughed at their English, and taunted them in the class and in the schoolyard. Gradually, more details were added until we formulated an outline.

Scene Outline: The Bullies at P.S. No. 1

> *Who:* Miss Malloy (the teacher), a principal, two recent immigrants (brother and sister), other immigrants, American children (nine to eleven)
>
> *Where:* classroom on the lower east side of New York City (circa 1910)
>
> *What* (the scenario as developed during improvisational sessions): Miss Malloy is leading the class through opening exercises. She is angry at the immigrants who are late or don't follow directions. An arithmetic lesson begins; some haven't done their homework. One immigrant, Anna, can't pronounce a word to the teacher's satisfaction. The American students laugh and jeer, making comments to the girl. The principal arrives, hearing the disturbance. She calls the teacher out. The teacher assigns spelling to be copied from the board. While the teacher is out, the bullies tease the girl. Her bother, Ivan, comes to her defense, standing up to the bullies. The verbal battle degenerates to a physical one. The teacher returns and stops the fight. The immigrant boy, lacking the vocabulary, is unsuccessful in explaining what happened. The immigrant is sent to the principal's office.

Linking the Past to the Present

Questions to consider: What groups of immigrants are arriving in America today? Why are they coming? Are their experiences in school any different from those of the children in the scene? How do you feel about immigrants? If you are a recent immigrant, how do you feel about how you are treated by Americans?

Playing the Scene

As the scene is played for the first time, I interject questions that help the students think about ways to reveal characters, setting, and the conflict to the audience. At times, I assume a role in the scene, in this case, Miss Malloy. Playing a character with a role of authority, I'm able to keep the action moving along. Mostly, I assume a position on the sideline, ready to coach if needed. Some of my side-coaching questions might be the following:

- How would you stand for the Pledge of Allegiance?
- How can you show that the class takes place in 1910?
- In what position would you sit at your desk?
- How can the bullies show that they are sneaky?
- How can the Americans show that they think the immigrants are inferior?
- How can you use your body to express what you are feeling?
- When the children laugh at you (immigrants), how do you react?
- How do the immigrant children show that they are embarrassed by their English?
- Is the teacher unsympathetic to the immigrants? How does she show it?

The Reflection

When the improvisation is finished, the students begin the reflection stage by responding to my questions. A number of general questions are listed earlier in the chapter and these are useful in most discussions. Some questions specific to this scene might be the following:

- Were the classroom activities believable?
- What activities can be added to establish the setting more clearly?
- Was the student behavior realistic for 1910?
- Was the conflict of discrimination too exaggerated? Does it need to be more subtle?
- Are there actions that the audience sees and the teacher doesn't?
- What does the audience need to know about the immigrant kids?
- How does the teacher's behavior influence the attitude of the class?

Replaying the Scene

In the replaying, students work to strengthen the central idea of the improvisation. Individuals work to build their characters and project an emotion to the audience. The reading of firsthand accounts by immigrants helps the students add substance to the scene and their character. These sample questions present new problems for the actors to solve before, during, and after the scene:

- How do you feel about the immigrant kids?
- What's going through your mind as they struggle to speak?
- Do you enjoy Ms. Malloy's class?

- Are you a good student?
- Do you like pleasing the teacher?
- When did your parents come to America? Are they doing well?
- Who are your friends in the class?
- Are you mean? Aggressive? Quiet? Talkative?
- Are you a leader in the class?
- Do you like attention from your classmates?
- What kind of a speaking voice can you create for yourself?
- What props might help create the setting?
- What costume piece would help reveal your character?
- How does your character move?
- How can the fighting boys make the fighting look real without hurting each other?
- Why does Miss Malloy behave in the way she does? Were her parents immigrants, too?

The Final Stage of the Process

I repeat the process until a tempo emerges that will hold the audience's attention and bring the scene to a timely climax. I know when we've reached this stage because I see that the students are working together as an ensemble, listening to each other, focusing on the action, and not trying to call attention to themselves. The following scene excerpt developed from the improvisational drama described here, and is scripted in play form to give the reader an example of a fully developed improvisational scene.

Scene: The Bullies at P.S. No. 1

(The students file in and take their seats in the class. The teacher follows.)

MISS MALLOY: (picks up a pointer from the desk and taps) Class! (At this signal, the students all rise and stand at attention for the Pledge of Allegiance.)

ALL STUDENTS: I pledge allegiance to the flag of the United States of America, and to the republic for which it stands, one nation, indivisible, with liberty and justice for all.

MISS MALLOY: And now for the morning exercises. Inhale . . . exhale . . . inhale . . . exhale. Hands on your shoulders, arms up, arms out, one, two, three, one, two, three, one (she notices a late student run in and try to get to his seat unnoticed). Anthony! Come here!

ANTHONY: Good morning, Miss Malloy, I'm sorry that I'm late but I didn't have . . .

MISS MALLOY: (interrupting) Anthony, this is the third time that you've been late this week. This can't go on!

ANTHONY: But, Miss Malloy, it's not my fault. I was hauling coal and my boss asked me to . . .

MISS MALLOY: (interrupting) I know about your boss and he's been told that all the children need to be on time for school. He's just greedy. Now, let me see your hands. (Anthony shows his black, dirty hands to the teacher.) Go to the boys room and wash them before you come back into this class! (Anthony runs out and Miss Malloy continues the exercises.) One, two, three, and one, two three, and one, two, three. (They finish the exercises.) Good morning, boys and girls.

ALL STUDENTS: (in a sing-song voice) Good morning, Miss Malloy.

MISS MALLOY: You may be seated class. (noticing a student in the back with his hat on) Johann!

JOHANN: (stands) Yes, Miss Malloy.

MISS MALLOY: Remove your hat.

JOHANN: Yes, Miss Malloy (sits down, but does not take off his hat).

MISS MALLOY: Johann! the hat! Take off the hat! (exasperated, she turns to another student) Bruno, please translate what I said to Johann.

JOHANN: (Bruno leans over and says something quietly in German, and Johann understands and immediately removes his hat.) Yes, Miss Malloy!

MISS MALLOY: Now we'll see who did their homework last night. Who can recite the three times table? (Many children raise their hand and call out Miss Malloy's name as she scans the room for unraised hands.) Thomas, you try it.

THOMAS: (stands) Three times one is three. Three times two is . . . ah . . . ah . . . six? Three times three is twelve. (some students laugh)

MISS MALLOY: Sit down, Thomas. It's obvious you didn't do your homework. So tonight you'll write the entire table one hundred times. (Miss Malloy continues to scan the room and sees a student sleeping. She taps her with a pointer.) Rosa! Rosa! Wake up! What's wrong with you, didn't you sleep last night?

ROSA: Not much, Miss Malloy.

MISS MALLOY: Were you helping your father with his work?

ROSA: Yes, Miss Malloy. We make cigars for long, long time, until morning almost.

MISS MALLOY: So, of course you didn't do your homework, is that right, Rosa? (Rosa shakes her head to indicate a "yes") Well, who did? (Many children raise their hand again, calling the teacher's name.) All right, Lillian, you try it.

LILLIAN: (stands with her hands behind her back and recites perfectly in a know-it-all voice) Three times one is three, three times two is six [and so on].

MISS MALLOY: Very well done, Lillian. Anna, did you do your homework?

ANNA: (timidly with a strong accent) Yes, Miss Malloy.

MISS MALLOY: Go on, then, recite.

ANNA: Tree time one is tree. Tree times two . . . (everyone in the class is laughing, except her brother Ivan)

MISS MALLOY: Anna, it's *three* times one is *three*.

ANNA: Tree times one is tree. (more laughter)

MISS MALLOY: Anna, a tree is a plant. Look (pointing to the street), that's a tree out there. It has leaves on it. *Three* is a number, like this (points to the number cards). *Three!* Say it!

ANNA: Tree. (more laughter)

Miss Malloy: Watch my mouth, you say it like this: *thr-e-e.*
Anna: (takes a long concentrated pause, trying to imitate Miss Malloy) Tree. (The laughter is now hysterical, and students are imitating Anna by saying "tree.")
Principal: (bursting through the door) What's the meaning of this commotion? Why aren't these students working? Miss Malloy, I'd like to speak with you in private.
Miss Malloy: Yes, Mrs. Childe. Children, please copy the spelling words from the board into your notebooks, ten times each! And not a sound out of anyone while I'm gone! (exits with the principal)

(The scene continues with the bullies of the class teasing Anna again until her brother Ivan intervenes. He defends his sister and tells them that she's not dumb. They continue until it escalates into a fight. The teacher reenters the scene, pulls apart the children, and they all scurry to their seats. She questions Ivan, but his English is not good enough to explain what happened, and the bullies convince Miss Malloy that it was Ivan's fault. Ivan gets sent to the principal's office.)

Assessment Strategies

Because students are engaged in a wide variety of learning activities in my social studies class, assessment strategies are equally varied to include *observation, paper and pencil tasks,* and *conferencing.* The ongoing evaluative techniques involving observation (both formal and informal) evident in this chapter are discussion and reflection, self-assessment, and informal performance. Paper and pencil tasks are used to evaluate completed research, encourage reflection, develop a dramatic character, and assess an understanding of the historical content. Conferencing is also used with individuals and groups to evaluate progress in research and problem solving.

When observing the drama/social studies improvisational process, I look at two major areas: discussion and performance. Discussion is an important part of any social studies class, so I try to evaluate how students are developing in this area. I look at their performance in an improvisation because, although I'm not training actors, the performance is part of the entire process. It is a cooperative learning activity with drama/social studies and language arts content. Therefore, it is valid to assess the performance. Informal observation takes place whenever we meet for an improvisational session. A more formal observation takes place when I watch a videotape of a drama session and use a checklist to assess student performance. A sample *observation checklist* of criteria is shown in Figure 3–2.

Resources

Selected Professional Resources for Improvisational Drama

Heathcote, D. & G. Bolton. 1995. *Drama for Learning.* Portsmouth, NH: Heinemann.
    Heathcote's mantle of expert approach is explained and applied to specific curriculum

Observation Checklist

Drama/Social Studies Improvisation

	consistent	developing	not evident
In discussion, the student			
1. participates in brainstorming, planning, decision making	_____	_____	_____
2. states opinion or suggestions clearly	_____	_____	_____
3. listens respectfully to others	_____	_____	_____
4. makes compromises to reach a consensus	_____	_____	_____
5. speaks meaningfully about historical content	_____	_____	_____
6. reflects and offers suggestions for revision	_____	_____	_____
In performance, the student			
1. listens to and follows directions	_____	_____	_____
2. listens to other players	_____	_____	_____
3. stays focused during entire performance	_____	_____	_____
4. works to develop a character	_____	_____	_____
5. moves with ease in the acting space	_____	_____	_____
6. projects voice	_____	_____	_____
7. articulates clearly	_____	_____	_____
8. works to make historical setting, character, and conflict believable	_____	_____	_____
9. demonstrates a perceptive use of props and costume pieces	_____	_____	_____

Figure 3–2. Observation Checklist. Drama/Social Studies Improvisation

areas. Several chapters focusing on history take the reader from the exploration with the teacher in role to the presentation.

McCaslin, N. 1996. *Creative Drama in the Classroom and Beyond,* 6th ed. White Plains, NY: Longman. This is an excellent reference because it covers all facets of creative drama for the classroom and performance for an audience. Chapters 6, 8, and 9 deal specifically with improvisation and building plays from literature. This book is well organized, easy to follow, and filled with practical ideas.

Salazar, G. 1995. *Teaching Dramatically Learning Thematically.* Charlottesville, VA: New Plays, Inc. Laura Gardner Salazar, although influenced by Heathcote, has her own style of drama. She introduces the thematic style in Chapter 1, gives the basics of thematic drama in Chapter 3, and moves on to a detailed account of thematic lessons, some of which focus on history, in the remaining chapters.

Stewig, J. & C. Buege. 1994. *Dramatizing Literature in Whole Language Classrooms,* 2nd ed. New York: Teachers College Press. This book does an excellent job of showing teachers, including those with no formal drama background, the how-to's of improvisational drama. There are helpful descriptions of literature-based drama experiences in which they describe motivational techniques, initiating scenes, the leader's role, redoing scenes, and dealing with problems.

Resources for "The Boston Massacre and Its Aftermath (1770)"

Bracken, J.M., ed. 1995. *The Shot Heard 'Round the World: The Beginnings of the American Revolution.* Carlisle, MA: Discovery Enterprises.

Brenner, B. 1994. *If You Were There in 1776.* New York: Simon & Schuster.

Dwyer, F. 1989. *John Adams.* New York: Chelsea House.

Hakim, J. 1993. *A History of Us: From Colonies to Country.* New York: Oxford University Press. (see Chapter 13: "A Massacre in Boston")

Phelan, M.K. 1976. *The Story of the Boston Massacre.* New York: Crowell.

Silverman, J. 1994. *Songs and Stories of the American Revolution.* Brookfield, CT: Millbrook Press.

Resources for "Willy Freeman Testifies in Court"

Collier, J.L. & C. Collier. 1981. *Jump Ship to Freedom.* New York: Dell Yearling.

Collier, J.L. & C. Collier. 1983. *War Comes to Willy Freeman.* New York: Dell Yearling.

Hakim, J. 1993. *A History of Us: From Colonies to Country.* New York: Oxford University Press. (see Chapter 39: "Good Words and Bad Words")

Hamilton, V. 1993. *Many Thousands Gone: African Americans from Slavery to Freedom.* New York: Alfred A. Knopf.

Resources for "In the Slave Quarters with Frederick Douglass"

Banta, M. 1993. *Frederick Douglass: Voice of Liberty.* New York: Chelsea Juniors.

Bennet, E. 1993. *Frederick Douglass and the War Against Slavery.* Brookfield, CT: Millbrook Press.

Bial, R. 1997. *The Strength of These Arms: Life in the Slave Quarters.* Boston: Houghton Mifflin.

Douglass, F. 1968. *Narrative of the Life of Frederick Douglass.* New York: Signet.

Erikson, P. 1997. *Daily Life on a Southern Plantation, 1853.* New York: Lodestar.

Hakim, J. 1994. *A History of Us: Liberty for All?* New York: Oxford University Press.

Hine, W.C. 1975. *Slavery in the United States, Jackdaw Portfolio no. A30.* Amawalk, NY: Golden Owl.

Lester, J. 1968. *To Be a Slave.* New York: Dial.

Lyons, M.E. 1992. *Letters from a Slave Girl.* New York: Atheneum.

McKissack, P. 1997. *A Picture of Freedom: The Diary of Clotee, a Slave Girl, Belmont Plantation, Virginia, 1859.* New York: Scholastic.

Meltzer, M. [1964] 1984. *The Black Americans: A History in Their Own Words, 1619–1983.* New York: HarperCollins.

Paulsen, G. 1993. *Nightjohn.* New York: Laurel Leaf.

———. 1997. *Sarny: A Life Remembered.* New York: Delacorte.

Weiner, E. 1992. *The Story of Frederick Douglass: Voice of Freedom.* New York: Dell Yearling.

Resources for "The Mill Girls Organize to Fight Poor Labor Conditions"

Avi. 1996. *Beyond the Western Sea, Book II: Lord Kirkle's Money.* New York: Avon Camelot.

Collier, J.L. & C. Collier. 1992. *The Clock.* New York: Yearling.

Colman, P. 1995. *Strike! The Bitter Struggle of American Workers from Colonial Times to the Present.* Brookfield, CT: Millbrook Press.

Denenberg, B. 1997. *So Far from Home: The Diary of Mary Driscoll, an Irish Mill Girl, Lowell, Massachusetts, 1847.* New York: Scholastic.

Dunwell, S. 1978. *Run of the Mill.* Boston: D.R. Godine.

Holland, R. 1970. *Mill Child.* London: Crowell Collier.

Macaulay, D. 1983. *Mill.* Boston: Houghton Mifflin.

McCully, E.M. 1996. *The Bobbin Girl.* New York: Dial.

Paterson, K. 1991. *Lyddie.* New York: Puffin.

Selden, B. 1983 *The Mill Girls: Lucy Larcom, Harriet Hanson Robinson, and Sarah G. Bagley.* New York: Atheneum.

Weisman, J.B., ed. 1991. *The Lowell Mill Girls: Life in the Factory.* Carlisle, MA: Discovery Enterprises.

Zimiles, M. & M. Zimiles. 1973. *Early American Mills.* New York: Clarkson N. Potter.

Resources for "Trouble Erupts at School over the Issue of Slavery (1851)"

Bland, C. 1993. *Harriet Beecher Stowe.* New York: Chelsea Juniors.

Davis, H. & N. Robinson. 1985. *History You Can See: Scenes of Change in Rhode Island, 1790–1910*. Providence, RI: Rhode Island Publication Society.

Emert, P.R., ed. 1995. *Colonial Triangular Trade: An Economy Based on Human Misery*. Carlisle, MA: Discovery Enterprises.

Fennessey, S. 1998. *The Loom and the Lash: A Play About a Family's Conflict During the Time of Southern Slavery and Northern Industrialization*. Carlisle, MA: Discovery Enterprises.

Hakim, J. 1994. *A History of Us: Liberty for All?* New York: Oxford University Press.

Katz, W.L. 1990. *Breaking the Chains: African American Slave Resistance*. New York: Aladdin.

McKissack, P.C. & F.L. McKissack. 1996. *Rebels Against Slavery: American Slave Protests*. New York: Scholastic. (see Chapter 6: "Rebel Abolitionists")

Nadalin, C.M. 1996. "The Last Years of the Rhode Island Slave Trade." *Rhode Island History* 54 (2): 35–49.

Stachiw, M.O. 1983. "For the Sake of Commerce: Rhode Island, Slavery, and the Textile Industry," an essay to accompany the exhibit, "The Loom and the Lash," at the Museum of Rhode Island History at Aldrich House.

Zeinert, K. 1997. *The Amistad Slave Revolt and American Abolition*. North Haven, CT: Linnet Books.

Resources for "The Orphans Are Placed Out"

Bracken, J.M., ed. 1997. *The Orphan Trains: Leaving the Cities Behind*. Carlisle, MA: Discovery Enterprises.

Holland, I. 1990. *The Journey Home*. New York: Scholastic.

Nixon, J.L. 1987. *A Family Apart*. New York: Dell.

Warren, A. 1996. *Orphan Train Rider: One Boy's True Story*. Boston: Houghton Mifflin.

Resources for "Langston Hughes Experiences Jim Crowism (circa 1917)"

Cryan-Hicks, K., ed. 1993. *Pride and Promise: The Harlem Renaissance*. Carlisle, MA: Discovery Enterprises.

Dunham, M. 1975. *Langston Hughes: Young Black Poet*. New York: Aladdin.

Hakim, J. 1995. *A History of Us: War, Peace, and All That Jazz*. New York: Oxford University Press.

Haskins, J. 1996. *The Harlem Renaissance*. Brookfield, CT: Millbrook Press.

Hughes, L. 1994. *The Dreamkeeper and Other Poems*. New York: Alfred A Knopf.

———. 1958. *The Langston Hughes Reader*. New York: George Braziller.

Meltzer, M. 1997. *Langston Hughes: An Illustrated Edition*. Brookfield, CT: Millbrook Press.

New York Center for Visual History. (Producer). 1988. *Voices and Visions: Langston Hughes #6*. [videotape]. New York: Annenberg/CPB Collection.

Rummel, J. 1988. *Langston Hughes: Poet*. New York: Chelsea House.

Taylor, M. D. 1976. *Roll of Thunder, Hear My Cry*. New York: Dial.

————. 1987a. *The Friendship*. New York: Dial.

————. 1987b. *The Gold Cadillac*. New York: Dial.

————. 1990. *Mississippi Bridge*. New York: Dial.

Trotter, J.W. Jr. 1996. *From Raw Deal to New Deal: African Americans, 1929–1945: The Young Oxford History of African Americans*, vol. 8. New York: Oxford University Press.

Resources for "Underground Resistance in World War II"

Hakim, J. 1995. *A History of Us: War, Peace, and All That Jazz*. New York: Oxford University Press.

Lowry, L. 1989. *Number the Stars*. New York: Dell.

Marks, J. 1993. *The Hidden Children: The Secret Survivors of the Holocaust*. New York: Fawcett Columbine.

McSwigan, M. 1942. *Snow Treasure*. New York: Apple Scholastic.

Meltzer, M. 1976. *Never to Forget: The Jews of the Holocaust*. New York: Harper & Row.

————. 1988. *Rescue: The Story of How Gentiles Saved Jews in the Holocaust*. New York: Harper Trophy.

Phillips, W. 1992. *The Holocaust: Jackdaw Portfolio no. G81*. Amawalk, NY: Golden Owl.

Reiss, J. 1972. *The Upstairs Room*. New York: Harper Trophy.

Richter, H.P. 1970. *Friedrich*. New York: Holt, Rinehart, and Winston.

Resources for "The Immigrant Experience"

Bales, C.A. 1977. *Tales of the Elders: A Memory Book of Men and Women Who Came to America As Immigrants, 1900–1930*. New York: Follett.

Blumenthal, S. 1981. *Coming to America: Immigrants from Eastern Europe*. New York: Delacorte.

Blumenthal, S. & J. Ozer. 1980. *Coming to America: Immigrants from the British Isles*. New York: Delacorte.

Emsden, K., ed. 1993. *Coming to America: A New Life in a New Land*. Carlisle, MA: Discovery Enterprises.

Freedman, R. 1980. *Immigrant Kids*. New York: Dutton.

Lasky, K. 1998. *Dreams in the Golden Country: The Diary of Zipporah Feldman, a Jewish Immigrant Girl, New York City 1903*. New York: Scholastic.

Mofford, J.H., ed. 1997. *Child Labor in America*. Carlisle, MA: Discovery Enterprises.

Nixon, J.L. 1994. *Land of Dreams*. New York: Delacorte.

————. 1992. *Land of Hope*. New York: Bantam.

————. 1993. *Land of Promise*. New York: Bantam.

Robbins, A. 1981. *Coming to America: Immigrants from Northern Europe*. New York: Delacorte.

Sandler, M.N. 1995. *Immigrants: A Library of Congress Book*. New York: HarperCollins.

4

The Performance: Sharing the Classroom Project

I learned how hard and easy it is to put on a play. But most of all, I learned really how to work together. If everyone works together, sings, claps, and helps, you can have a wonderful performance, and we did. I loved the play.

Yann, age 10

About twenty years ago, I staged my first historical drama production with a fifth grade class. The entire school gathered in the gym to celebrate Martin Luther King Day. My students presented three scenes strung together with narration: the Rosa Parks bus incident, the Montgomery bus boycott, and a sit-in at a "Whites Only" lunch counter. Using these historic moments as ideas for improvisations in class, my original intention was simply to help the children understand Jim Crow laws and the idea of nonviolent protest. But as we worked on the improvisations in class, I recognized their potential for performance. At this point, I made the decision to bring them to performance level for presentation to an audience of their peers. This meant that the improvisational drama had to move into the realm of theatre. What happens in that process is the subject of this chapter.

Staging a performance is a big undertaking and may not be for everyone. Drama can be used as a successful teaching strategy without ever getting out of the classroom and onto a stage, but I have found that a performance is an extremely worthwhile project and a way to share classroom learning with others. Each year my students and I make a considerable time commitment to preparing and performing an historical play for the school. In the all-encompassing role of the director, I prepare the script, cast the play, stage the movement, guide the young actors to develop their characters, choose a suitable performance place, and prepare scenery, props, lighting, and costumes. The students become responsible for learning lines, memorizing blocking, taking care of scenery, props, lighting, and costume changes, and all the while being cooperative, disciplined, and attentive listeners.

Although a production is considerable work, I view it as the next natural step for students who have been involved for many months in using drama as a way of constructing meaning for history. Usually by the second half of the school year, the students have developed the ability to work together in a disciplined way. They are comfortable speaking and moving in our drama circle and are ready to make the transition to a theatrical performance. There are some in the field of drama, however, who say that children should not perform because they do little more than imitate adults. This is not necessarily true. If the performance is an outgrowth of an integrated social studies project, and if the students have developed an understanding of the core ideas of the play through improvisational drama, then the next natural step is a performance. I've observed that it's justified in other disciplines as well. Student artwork adorns the halls of schools or is presented at special exhibits. Music students perform in concert for parents and other students. The performance is a way for students to share what they've learned in class. So why not in drama? I see it as the final step in the process described so far in this book. It's not a necessary step, but a particularly rewarding one, especially for the students involved. What follows is a description of the process involved in the planning, rehearsing, and performance of an historical play.

With a Performance Comes a Responsibility

The informal dramatic pieces that we've developed in classroom sessions cannot be transferred, as is, into a formal theatre production. As the director, I have a responsibility, along with the young actors, to create a theatre experience for the audience. The nature of theatre demands that the production be an enjoyable one, involving the audience vicariously in the lives and emotions of people from the past. Theatre (with a combination of the elements of scenery, lighting, costumes, staging, the script, and actors) should also fully engage the audience's attention. When presenting a performance, I aim for the best quality production, considering what I have available to me as resources.

Creating or Selecting a Play for Performance

The plays presented by my class are the culminating activity of a social studies unit. Sometimes, I develop the play from the work we've done during the drama/history improvisational sessions, building on those scenes, as well as adding new ones. At other times, I've written much of the script before we begin the unit; then the improvised scenes are developed in class, scripted, and added to the drama. When the scenes are ready to be scripted, I write down the dialogue created in the drama sessions. We read it together, and suggestions for additions or deletions are made by the students and me. Older students, especially upper middle school, can write their own scripts along with the teacher. The content of the entire play is largely based on the historical improvisations created in class and brought to a performance level through revision sessions. To these core scenes I might add introductory narration or create a prologue or epilogue. Finally, I ask myself what other information the audience needs to know about the plot. Then, additional scenes are added for clarity, to reveal more about the lead characters to the audience, or simply to keep the action moving along. (See the *In the Spotlight* section at the end of this chapter for a detailed description of how one class project evolved into a play.)

When it's not possible to develop a play with the class, I need to select something suitable from available play scripts. Choices are limited, which is why I originally started writing plays. Often the language is too unnatural to suit the rhythm of children's speech patterns, the situations are corny, or the characters aren't developed. There are a number of publishers who specialize in children's plays and lately have included scripts that deal with historical events or people. (See Resources at the end of this chapter for suggestions.)

Whether I'm building my own play based on scenes developed in the classroom or choosing one from a catalogue, there are some questions that I consider regarding the script:

- Does the plot have sufficient action and variety of scenes to sustain the interest of the audience?
- Does the major problem or conflict move the plot forward, keeping the action alive on stage?
- Are the main characters interesting people with whom the audience can identify?
- Does the language of the script communicate simply and clearly to the audience?
- Does the dialogue capture the emotions and substance of the main characters?
- Does the script say what we want it to say to the audience?
- Is it a worthwhile message?
- Does the script show (through dramatic action) rather than tell (say it) the theme to the audience?
- Can the play be cast appropriately (especially the lead)?
- Are there parts for all students to participate in some capacity?
- Are there any special scenery or costume problems that present too much of a challenge for the resources available?

Developing a Performance: Three Major Considerations

Some subjects are better suited to dramatization than are others. Consider, for example, the life of Martin Luther King, Jr. As a lead character, he is a protagonist who is a true hero, and his life touches the lives of others who also had the courage of their convictions. They, too, provide additional interesting characters for a play. His life is a series of dramatic events, providing the framework for a plot and the theme of civil rights. When developing a script, I consider three elements: plot, theme, and characters.

Plot

The plot is the story, the basic structure within which the characters interact. It needs to grow logically to a climax and come to a satisfying conclusion. It also needs to have sufficient action and change of scene to sustain the interest of a young audience. In a Martin Luther King project developed several years ago, our plot was built from four improvisations created in class and based on research and readings on King's life:

- The Shoe Store Incident (Young Martin, Jr., goes to buy shoes with his father, and the salesman insists that they sit in the back section of the shoe store. Rev. King, Sr., refuses and they leave the store without buying shoes.)
- Rosa Parks on the Bus (Rosa Parks, while riding on a Montgomery, Alabama, city bus, is told by the bus driver that she must give up her seat to a white passenger. She refuses to do so. Police are called and Parks is arrested. The Montgomery bus boycott begins.)
- The Lunch Counter Sit-In (King and some black students stage a sit-in at a "Whites Only" lunch counter. They are insulted and abused by the white patrons. When they refuse to leave, police are called, and they are arrested for trespassing.)
- The Washington March (At a huge demonstration in Washington, DC, King delivers his famous "I Have A Dream" speech. The crowd shouts out civil rights slogans. They sing "We Shall Overcome.")

From these scenes, a skeletal plot emerged on which more dramatic action was built until the entire plot structure was complete.

Theme

A good play should dramatize (show) not state (tell) the message. In the King play, for example, the audience saw the characters struggling to overcome the obstacles of racism. The thematic material—African Americans were denied basic civil rights—was revealed through the actions and language of the characters.

The scenes I've listed contained enough action and variety to provide the basis for the scenario. I then created additional scenes to help move the plot forward smoothly and unify the production. For instance, a scene took place in an Alabama courtroom where King is sentenced to six months in a federal penitentiary. It provided a dramatic moment in which the audience realizes that King was ready to be jailed for his beliefs and that the Alabama court punished King (for a minor offense of trespassing) to the fullest extent of the law as a deterrent example to other African Americans.

Characters

Characters need to be believable. The audience should get to know the characters on stage, care about them, and be moved emotionally by them. King is a rich character, a man with a vision, yet human and vulnerable to attack by those who hated him. He makes an ideal protagonist. In the scenes I've listed here, a variety of major and minor characters interact with King in the script. In addition to Martin Luther King, Jr. (as a boy and as an adult) there was Rev. King, Sr., Alberta King (the mother), Rosa Parks, Ralph Abernathy, the judge, and a wide spectrum of minor characters, including demonstrators, bus riders, people at the lunch counter, civil rights marchers, and so on. In essence, there were parts for everyone in my class, with some actors portraying two or three characters.

Theatrical Devices Used to Reveal Plot, Theme, and Character

When I'm building a play script, I rely on a repertoire of devices to pull the performance together and communicate meaning to the audience. I also try to keep the play moving along with frequent action and scene changes, and a running time of one hour or less, which suits young audiences. In various productions, I've tried some of the techniques listed here.

Narration

To bridge time and place, I sometimes connect scripted scenes with narration performed by the students acting as the storytellers of the past, relating the history unfolding before the audience. Most plays don't use narration, but because historical plays chronicle true events in a person's life, or an historical period, narration is a useful device. I sometimes write the narration myself, or if we have the time, I write the narration with the kids. If this is the case, then during the writer's conference, I ask, "What does the audience need to know at this point in the play?" "How can we move from this point in time to that?" As we confer, we work to keep the narrator's lines short, in simple, direct language that is stimulating to an audience of young listeners. Too much narration is deadly. In the King project, the narration was a useful device because events in the life of King took place during an extended period of time.

Characters Speak to the Audience

At the beginning or at the end of a scene, the actor leaves center stage, stepping out of the scripted role, and walks closer to the audience, speaking directly to them.

This device can be used to comment on the action or communicate new information to the audience. For example, in a play we performed on the life of Frederick Douglass, the character of Douglass frequently spoke to the audience, sharing his feelings about his slavemasters.

The Flashback Technique

The flashback is a device used to show the audience an event that happened before the play. In the King production, I used the flashback technique to bring action to a story. Alberta King, Martin's mother, explains to six-year-old Martin why African Americans, although free, were still denied their basic rights. As a bedtime story, she reads from *The Narrative of the Life of Frederick Douglass*. As Martin listens, he questions his mother: "How did he (Douglass) become a slave?" As the mother begins to answer the question, the lights fade, and the audience is transported to an African village. Dance and mime tell the story of their journey from freedom to slavery. (See *Tableaux* and *Tableaux Variation* in Chapter 2 for an example of this mime/movement activity.)

Prologue and Epilogue

The prologue introduces the play to the audience. Not all historical plays need a prologue, but I find it a useful device for communicating information to an audience that may not have the knowledge base necessary (due to their age) to understand the time, place, and circumstances surrounding the events in the play. In the King play, the prologue was performed through a song we wrote, as well as through narration. An excerpt from the lyrics generated by the students is as follows:

> Come listen to me, and I'll sing you a song,
> Of a man they called Martin, so determined and strong.
> He led marches in peace, saying "we shall overcome"
> while the people were singing of freedom.

An epilogue closes a play. Its function is to tie up all the loose ends for the audience. Few plays use this device, but in the example of the King play, the epilogue showed the audience what events took place in his life after the Washington March. It was accomplished with slides and live voice-over narration. We chose slides that documented important marches, time in jail, the passage of civil rights laws, and the assassination. The audience responded enthusiastically to this part of the performance. Reflecting on it afterward, I thought that it was perhaps the sudden change of pace and the introduction of the new medium that caught the audience's attention.

The Integration of Music, Dance, and Art

I believe that the inclusion of music, dance, and art is an important addition to an historical project of this nature. The arts are an expression of a particular culture

71

and time, and they can be woven into the framework of the script, enriching the scenes with a flavor of the period. Besides helping to convey time and mood, music and dance reveal the humaneness of the characters, provide variety in the action for the audience, and give the ensemble more time on stage.

Music fit naturally and historically into our study of the Civil Rights Movement of the 1950s and 1960s. Protest and freedom songs were sung at demonstrations, marches, and boycotts. A song such as "We Shall Not Be Moved" enhanced the mood of the bus boycott, and the song "We Shall Overcome" signified the power of the people assembled at the Washington March.

Through dance, the students employ their kinesthetic intelligence, using their bodies to understand and communicate ideas. I have found that folk dance is useful in a colonial history project, for example, to help students understand some aspects of society in eighteenth-century colonial America. While learning the minuet, students experience the formality of a court dance via deep bows, curtseys, gloved hands, slow and even movements, and erect postures to maintain the position of powdered fancy wigs. Participating in such a dance reveals a lot about the social conventions of that time, and provides a startling contrast to today's style of social dance. Just to compare the two styles reveals an extraordinary amount of information about both societies.

Creative movement is another way to communicate an idea to the audience. Without words, the actors reveal ideas, events, and emotional experiences through the language of the body. In the King project, I used dance movement in a flashback sequence to give a suggestion of African culture at the time of the slave trade. Mime and movement helped characterize a ritual dance ceremony. Masks, created in art class and inspired by the study of African art, were worn by the dancers.

Choral Speaking as a Theatrical Device

Choral speaking can be a very powerful theatrical device. The actors recite in unison or divide into groups to give texture to the performance. A chorus can be used in several different ways:

- It can comment on the action in the drama.
- It can provide sound effects for a scene in which establishing a mood is important.
- It can be combined with movement to reveal new information to the audience.

In the Langston Hughes play project (see Chapter 3), we wanted the plot to include something about Langston's experiences while traveling in West Africa. The question was, "How could this be managed in one scene?" The solution to the problem was found in the poetry written by Hughes while he was in Africa. His impressions of the country were expressed in poems like *African Dance*. The poem

Figure 4–1. Movement Is Integrated into Historical Projects

was chanted by a chorus of actors, drums were added, and dancers whirled rhythmically around an imaginary fire. The choral reading and the movement communicated to the audience the feelings that inspired Hughes to write the poem, and as a result, the audience had a more in-depth look at the poet's work.

Performance Space

Once the script is ready, I set a date and time and find a place for the class to perform. A small stage with a few spotlights is ideal. I try to avoid a large theatre with a big, elevated proscenium stage because it overwhelms the children, dwarfing them with its size and making it difficult for them to project. An all-purpose room, provided it has good acoustics, is also a possibility. I usually mask off the acting space and seat the audience close to the performers. A horseshoe-shaped playing area allows the audience to sit on three sides, with the fourth side used for scenery, entrances, and exits. It has the advantage of bringing the actors closer to the audience, allowing it to see and hear everything (especially important if the audience is composed largely of children). Normally, elevation is not needed, but to create different levels for a particular setting, I've used platforms or cube-shaped boxes. The classroom can also be used as a performance area. Although not ideal, due to its size and lack of lighting, with a little work and imagination, it can be turned into a playing area. I darken the room with shades, use several portable lights on stands, set up folding screens on the sides of the playing space to fashion an offstage area for entrances and exits. We push the desks aside, and the audience sits on rows of chairs or on the floor, depending on the age of the playgoers.

Blocking the Movement

When the site has been chosen, I then plan the physical arrangement of the actors on stage and their movement from place to place. This is called "blocking" a play. To work out a plan, I first decide where the scenery, platforms, exits, entrances, and so on, will be located on the stage in relation to the actors. Preplanning the blocking saves time at rehearsals. Adjustments can be made after the movement is tested and unforeseen problems arise. Committing their blocking to memory early in the rehearsal stage allows the young actors to move naturally around the stage after several weeks, and then focus attention on developing their character. When planning the blocking, I try to do the following:

- Make sure the speaking actor is visible to the audience and can be heard, especially when delivering an important line.
- Compose a stage picture that is visually balanced with a center of attention. A main character who is speaking needs to be emphasized visually and to be the focus of attention for the audience.
- Vary the body positions and levels of the actors. There are many ways to position the actors, but with young actors, the strongest positions for projection purposes are full-front or a quarter turn to the right or left. To vary the level, actors might sit, stand on steps or another type of elevation, lie down, kneel, slouch, lean, or just change the position of the head.
- Keep the blocking simple and functional. If the young actors have too much movement to remember, their focus will be taken away from their lines. I've also observed that they sometimes have difficulty walking and delivering a line at the same time, or singing while dancing. Moving just for the sake of variety will appear unnatural to the audience. The actors should be able to move with a purpose, easily find their place on stage, move to the next position, and smoothly make entrances and exits.

Casting the Play

I make sure that there are suitable roles for all students when creating a play or choosing one. I cast everyone in an on-stage role and stress the importance of each cast member for the success of the production. Everyone in the cast is also responsible for backstage work such as moving scenery, caring for props, or making sound effects. Once cast, the actors work to improve their characters. As the director, and also the classroom teacher, I have an advantage in the casting process. After months of working with the students in class on improvisational drama, I've identified each of the students' talents: who speaks clearly and loudly, who moves with confidence and grace, who works to develop a character, who is responsible and treats the process seriously, as well as the physical attributes of each student. In a situation such as this, tryouts are usually not necessary. If I'm undecided about the choice of a main character, however, I might have limited tryouts to find the best person for each major role. When the play is an outgrowth of a social studies project involving improvisational drama, the students are already very familiar with some of the scenes and the characters. With that familiarity comes a strong sense of who would be best suited to the major roles.

When announcing the casting choices, I always stress the importance of each and every role as being a crucial part of the entire production. Teamwork is the most important factor in a successful performance. Each actor must understand that as a part of the ensemble, he or she has a responsibility to the rest of the cast.

Rehearsals

Once a performance date has been set and the play is cast, I begin rehearsals without delay. Working with intermediate-age children, I like to have short rehearsals daily, because long sessions tire them. They lose focus and become restless. Rehearsals take place in the classroom drama area, but as the performance nears, we move to the stage. At this point, the students need to get their blocking oriented to the new space.

The entire process of preparing a performance takes between five and eight weeks. If it takes longer than eight weeks, I find that the young actor becomes bored with the material, character growth dissipates, and lines become rote recitations. I try to structure rehearsals to provide a variety of activity and include large and small group work. For example, I schedule scenes that require the entire cast, along with scenes involving two or three characters. Then, while I work with the small group, the remainder of the class is involved in self-directed activities. Doing library research, writing, reading, learning lines, and creating props, posters, and publicity materials are some of the ways that the children might be engaged while I work with the actors.

Early on in the rehearsal process, I try to block scenes that use the entire cast, because they require time, patience, and energy for all involved. Scenes that need choreography (for example, a fight scene or people at a fair), songs with movement, or folk dance, I also tackle at the start. This allows the kids time to feel comfortable with all the activity in the scene. Before I go into rehearsal, I plan the blocking of these scenes, songs, or dances in every detail. I know where everyone will be at any given moment in a song or dance or during the dialogue. I use floor plans of the stage, with the position of each actor marked, to help me during the rehearsal. In this way, I move quickly through the stage directions at rehearsals, and it prevents the students from losing their focus. Kids just don't wait quietly while I think about what to do next, so I've learned to be prepared with my stage drawings of little stick people and directions written down. If the students' concentration is on the wane, I change the activity by working on a different scene. The play is rehearsed in pieces up until two weeks before the performance. Then the actors perform the play in entirety to get a feeling of the continuity, the timing, and the logistics of scene changes.

A quality performance depends a great deal on my expectations as the teacher–director. At rehearsals, I challenge students to reach their potential. I treat the kids as actors (novices), using the professional language of the theater. I insist that they show respect for each other by being quiet while other actors are speaking. This sets the tone and builds a working atmosphere at rehearsals. Children easily comprehend the language of the stage. After several rehearsals, they are familiar with the jargon: "move downstage, stay in character, don't upstage the other actor, project your voice, quarter turn to the right," and so forth.

I also encourage students to develop their character. Through the research and improvisational work done in class, they already have some insight into knowing what motivates their character. To develop the actor's sense of character even further, I try some of the following activities:

- Students write a biography of their character, including typical actions and personality traits.
- Assuming the role of their character, students write entries in a diary.
- Students conduct an interview with another character in role.

Actors will use this knowledge to add more detail to their movements or gestures, use inflection in their voices, or simply put in a pause. The aim is to challenge the student–actor to make the character real, and eventually become the character.

Through the rehearsal process, children need both praise and criticism to develop their confidence. When offering comments, I keep them specific. I acknowledge when an actor does something well: "That cross looked good; keep it." "Your voice really made me believe that you were that person." "The dance had a lot of spirit today." When offering constructive criticism, I also keep the suggestions specific. I describe to the actor what needs to be done to improve: "Your inflection was good, but it's still not loud enough for the audience to hear." "A good gesture, but if you use your downstage arm, the audience will be able to see it better." "The steps to the dance are correct, but now you need to show the audience how you feel; convey the idea of a happy celebration."

During the entire rehearsal process, concentration and discipline are needed. I tell the actors to think about what they are saying and to listen carefully to the other actors. Students in the class who are musicians, dancers, or athletes understand that it takes practice and discipline to be successful in the arts or in sports.

Every rehearsal should have a purpose. Before the rehearsal starts, I gather the actors and state the purpose of the rehearsal, making clear the goals for the day. For example, I might announce, "Today we'll work on Scene One. We need to pick up the pace of the slave auction, and add the slave's jig with music." Actors also need to be given something to think about at the end of the rehearsal, so they can practice, revise, and try something new at the next rehearsal.

Props, Scenery, Costumes, Lighting, and Sound

I always put the kids to work backstage. I find that having the responsibility for the preparation, care, and operation of the technical elements of the production is something they enjoy, and has its purpose in the overall educational experience of putting on a performance. By involving the students, it

- emphasizes the necessity of teamwork
- demonstrates the importance of the technical elements to create the theater experience
- keeps students busy with backstage tasks (there is no time for socializing)
- teaches them to handle with respect the props, scenery, and costumes that took time and effort to prepare
- allows the various intelligences of the actor to be employed and valued

The *properties* (or *props,* as they are commonly called) needed for the production are collected at the start of the rehearsal stage. This gives the students practice working with them. After years of directing performances, I can find most props right in my classroom. I save items that I think could be useful, and people now give me things for props, as well as costumes. The kids refer to my closets as a "mini-mall," because whenever they ask me for something, I can usually produce it. Occasionally, some very special items are needed, and for these, I reach out to the school community. If parents and teachers are alerted early as to the needs of the production, most props usually can be found. Some will need to be made. This can sometimes be coordinated with the art teacher or a parent with artistic talent. Papier-mâché, aluminum foil, gold spray paint, cardboard or wood cutouts, and a little imagination can create simple yet effective props.

Figure 4–2. Students Prepare Props for a Play Production

Because all of the students will be working with props, I make clear my expectations. Early on in the year, I stress that "props are to be used in a play and not played with." With this phrase in mind, the young actors treat props carefully, returning them to the prop table when leaving the stage or rehearsal area. A few students with organizational talents are responsible for keeping track of the props with a checklist, and for making sure that the actors have the props needed on stage.

I try to keep *scenery* simple, just enough to suggest time, place, and mood. Scenery needs to be easy for the students to move on and off the stage, strong enough to stand firmly on its own, and skillfully yet simply executed. Most of our scenery is made from heavy-duty cardboard boxes. As "queen of the refrigerator box" (as I've come to be known), I can attest to the fact that they are free, sturdy, easy to transport, and take tempera paint well. Large rolls of brown paper (grocery bag quality) are used for backdrops. Frames with curtains hung on them roll on and off the stage to create an instant wall or a door for an entrance or exit. Cubes, arranged in different patterns or levels, also help create a setting. When I want to designate a particular locale, I might use steps or platforms. Designs projected onto a rear wall also create an instant backdrop. With little or no budget, I've had to be creative in coming up with low-cost possibilities to solve scenery problems for a production. I suspect that this would be the situation for most teachers. However, with the collaborative ideas of the classroom and school community, we usually achieve an appropriate and effective setting.

For young actors, *costumes* are one of the most exciting aspects of a play production. A costume confirms and legitimizes their characters. In a military jacket, the young actor becomes a soldier with an erect bearing. A long dress, petticoats, and a fan in the hand of a girl transforms her into an elegant eighteenth-century lady. I have found that it doesn't take much more than a simple accessory, such as a hat, a vest, shiny buttons, a tie, or a fur collar, to change an ordinary pair of trousers and shirt into a period boy's costume. I often use a long skirt and white blouse as the base for a girl's period outfit, to which I add accessories such as a shawl, a bonnet, and a pair of white gloves. Costuming an historical drama requires a little research to determine the typical mode of dress worn at the time the play is set. Once that is determined, I aim to have all the costumes suggest that period, a social class, or an occupation.

With a little imagination, just about any costume can be created with a few basics. I don't have a sewing machine, a budget to buy material, or a costume department to sew for us. So, I usually enlist the help of the students with the gathering and preparation of costumes. Once we have determined the style, I ask them to check their attics, closets, and basements for unused items that fit the description. I also find that yard sales, garage sales, flea markets, rummage sales, and thrift stores are great places to find clothing items that can be purchased for almost nothing and then stored to build a costume collection for use in class and in productions. When choosing basic pieces for use as costumes, I consider the overall color scheme because I want to have the costume colors blend, and avoid having them clash with the scenery.

The *lighting* is important for creating a mood, lighting the actors, and letting the audience know that a scene change will take place. Lighting is also helpful to designate a specific area on stage where the acting is taking place, or to create a special effect. It is perhaps the most important of the technical elements, but the one that I find the least manageable due to the lack of equipment and know-how.

When stage lights are not available, usually because we are performing in the classroom, I try to find creative alternatives. Some of the solutions that I've used in the past are flood lights or scoop lights (purchased at a hardware or discount store, or borrowed) for general lighting, or an overhead projector, equipped with a circular cardboard cutout, for a follow spot.

If stage lights are available, I make sure they are mounted securely and safely away from students. I leave the operation of lighting to an adult, but it is possible for students to operate a dimmer board and follow simple cues, such as "fade up" or "fade out."

Recorded *sound*, such as music, sets the mood before the play or during a scene. It camouflages the noise of a scene change or creates a special effect. I always record special sound effects (for example, an explosion, train whistle, baby's cries, etc.) ahead of time and rehearse them. I choose a student with technical talent to operate the tape recorder and listen for the appropriate cues, someone who'll assume the job of sound technician with pride and precision. Sound effects at the wrong moment can detract from the mood and attentiveness of the audience, and disrupt the actor's concentration.

Technical and Dress Rehearsals

At the technical and dress rehearsals, the scenery, lighting, costumes, props, and actors are integrated. Young actors need time and practice to deal with the new elements. The first time the stage lights are used, all the kids are squinting and complaining that they can't see anything. When the girls first start wearing long skirts, they need to experience walking and dancing in them to feel entirely comfortable. Time is needed to make adjustments on costumes that are uncomfortable or restrict the actors' movements. We practice quick costume changes during two or three rehearsals.

At this time, the actor–stagehands also rehearse the scene changes. I make a game out of it, timing them to improve the speed and accuracy of the changes. I emphasize safety factors first, as well as the importance of moving silently. Each of the "silent movers" knows their responsibilities and tries to meet them every time. I expect that the first technical rehearsal will be somewhat confusing for the kids and they are likely to make mistakes, forgetting scenery or costume pieces. But after we run through the changes a few times, they are proud of their ability to set the stage and make costume changes with such professionalism.

At these final rehearsals, I stage a curtain call and we practice it several times to achieve a professional look for the closing of the play. I aim for something simple that emphasizes the ensemble, rather than individuals.

The Performance

On the day of the performance, the students are charged with energy. The presence of an audience makes them nervous. It's my job to contain the excitement and reassure the students with words of encouragement. Running a smooth performance with children can be tricky. I take the time to personally check everything several hours before the performance, making sure all the scenery is in place and in operating condition. I go through the prop list to see if they are all on the prop table. I test the sound system, reviewing the cues for sound effects. With the help of parents, the costumes have been ironed and hang ready on a rack. As the kids walk to the performance space, they are excited and perhaps a little worried. I'm confident that they will all do fine because they have rehearsed well, and I have empowered them to assume responsibility during the performance for themselves, props, scenery, and costumes. Now they'll share what they know with an audience.

A realization of a good performance is achieved with teamwork. At this point, when the lights come up and the first actor speaks, everyone must rely on everyone else. Students instinctively know that this is a crucial element for success, and as the performance progresses, I see them helping each other with scenery, props, and costumes. I overhear kids reminding others to get ready for an entrance or to pick up a needed prop. Observing this, I'm overwhelmed with satisfaction because they're the best they can be and are all working toward a common goal. As a teacher, I couldn't ask for more. One fifth grade student in my class expressed her feelings on the subject in this way:

> Lucky for us we had teamwork. If I couldn't find my shirt, my friend would help me find it. If someone lost her shawl, we would be there to help her. When we arrived at the ballroom (the playing space), nervously the cast all did deep breathing and had a huddle. We put all our hands in and we raised them, shouting "good luck" and "break a leg." After that huddle, it seemed that we gained our confidence.

Andrea, age 10

I've included two checklists: one for the director and one for the actor. I use these lists to help me and the students have a smooth-running performance.

For the Director

- Check the sound system levels before the performance.
- Check to see that all props are on the prop table, or in the places where needed.
- Check scenery for any potential problems, especially support structure.
- Check the actors' costumes for any potential problems, such as a ripped seam, torn hem, spots, and so forth.
- Enlist the help of adults to supervise backstage, assist with fast costume changes and emergencies, and maintain a quiet work atmosphere.
- Equip the backstage crew with scripts that have lighting, sound, or scene-change cues marked.
- Avoid any last-minute changes in the technical elements or blocking, because they will make the actors more nervous.
- Above all, be calm, patient, smiling, unflappable, and prepared for anything. Equip yourself with emergency supplies such as duct tape, scissors, safety pins, flashlight, paper towels, and so forth.

For the Actor

- Keep a quiet working atmosphere backstage to allow the audience, actors, and stage crew to concentrate.
- Avoid peeking out or standing in view of the audience.
- Keep clear of moving scenery.
- Return all props to the designated prop table.
- Never eat or drink while in costume.
- Stay in character regardless of what happens (forgotten lines, falling scenery, a missing prop, etc.). Keep going, make up a line, and remember that the audience doesn't know the script.

The Audience

Without an audience, there is no performance. The playgoers are crucial to the success of the theatre experience. We usually invite all the students in the school whose ages range from four to twelve. Parents and relatives are also sprinkled throughout the audience. Kids need practice being attentive, listening carefully, showing respect for the actors, and generally observing good manners. The more they attend theatre, the better they behave. Some students have never been in a theatre and are unaware of the conventions, but if most of the audience is modeling correct playgoer behavior (listening attentively, applauding in the right places), the others catch on quickly.

It helps young audiences to know a little about the plot ahead of time. I send information about the play to all the teachers a few weeks before the performance. This might include a synopsis of scenes, background information on the historical events, characters, and suggestions for picture books on the topic. The teachers prepare the students for what they are about to see. Students who attend the play performance can expect to enjoy good theatre and benefit by the historical ideas revealed in the narrative drama. Sometimes, kids in the audience are inspired to create a play in their own class, or to attend another play in the future. The following excerpts are from letters written to my class by members of the audience responding to the play performance.

> I have learned a lot more about Harriet Tubman. I never knew that Harriet Tubman brought that many slaves to freedom. I never knew that so many things went into one production like the props, lights and costumes.
>
> Lindsay, age 9
>
> The play was informative and funny. My favorite scene was the wedding celebration. I liked all of the singing and dancing. Congratulations on the play and all your hard

work. I hope you can do another play and we can come see it. Maybe someday my class can do a play, and you can come see it!

Nicole, age 10

I thought your play was terrific! Truly, I've never seen anything quite like it. I'm one who personally loves history, especially about slaves, civil wars, and stuff like that. So for me to sit and watch a reenactment of a famous slave makes me happy. Even the accents were on point.

Dave, age 10

I learned a lot about slavery in Rhode Island. The scene where Daniel was teasing the man with the letter was very interesting. I liked to see my friends in your classroom acting on a big stage with a lot of people in the audience.

Eugene, age 9

It was probably neat to get to be somebody else for a little bit. I liked all of the characters. It was neat to see the same person that played different characters and didn't have the same clothes on.

Joslin, age 9

Figure 4–3. Students Learn to Concentrate and Work Cooperatively

The Performance as a Valuable Learning Experience

The performance has many educational values beyond those cited for classroom drama. Most obvious to me is the development of group cooperation and individual self-confidence. Students set aside individual differences for the sake of a common goal. Those with low self-esteem find success onstage while gaining new confidence in their offstage role of student. Other outcomes that I've observed are the following:

Social Development

- Students mature with the responsibility of running a production. Problem solving and on-the-spot decision making are commonplace.
- Concentration and self-discipline improve as they listen for cues, memorize lines and blocking, work to develop a character, move scenery, handle props, and operate lights.
- Interpersonal and intrapersonal intelligences are developed through the play experience.

Speech and Language Skills

- Students learn how to use their voices to capture the attention of the audience by using pauses and varying inflection and volume level.
- They practice diction and projection to communicate the message to the audience.
- The expressive language of the play enriches the vocabulary of the actors.
- Written language skills are enhanced for those involved in script writing.

Movement Skills and Coordination

- Actors learn control as they move from one place to another on stage, change body positions, use gestures and various postures, or participate in song, dance, and movement.
- Coordination is refined through dance, pantomime, choreographed movement, and blocking.

An Appreciation of Theatre as an Art

- Students recognize that theatre is a collaborative art, encompassing a wide range of elements.
- They gain knowledge of various forms of theatre, performance conventions, and styles.
- By experiencing good theatre, students develop a desire to attend live theatre performances.

In the Spotlight: The Civil Rights Movement

The Civil Rights Movement of the 1950s and 1960s happened long before the current elementary and middle school students were born. To become acquainted with this movement that brought conflict and change to American lives, I planned for the students to participate in a wide variety of activities, which included reading, writing, research, drama, song, dance, viewing videotapes and slides, and interviewing. As students immersed themselves in these activities, especially drama, my objective was to have them acquire some of the following understandings:

- African Americans were denied their basic civil rights.
- Laws and customs made it difficult for African Americans to succeed.
- Racism can move people to violence and extreme behavior.
- Individuals, groups, and institutions can make changes in society.
- Strategies used to bring about change were boycotts, sit-ins, demonstrations, marches, and passive resistance.
- The Civil Rights Movement of the 1950s and 1960s is the continuation of a long struggle connected to slavery, the framing of the Constitution, the Civil War, and the two world wars.

Motivation

In the fifth grade project cited here, a speaker was invited to the class, someone the children respected and knew well as a member of the school community. She told them stories, personal accounts of her childhood experiences with discrimination in the South. Her vivid descriptions of racist incidents generated a multitude of questions from the students as they interviewed her afterward. This activity launched research groups as the students formulated questions about their topics of interest:

- Who were prominent leaders in the Civil Rights Movement?
- What were the major events in King's life?
- What was the Montgomery bus boycott, and why did it work?
- How did Jim Crow laws affect the everyday lives of blacks in the South?
- How did Southern whites react to school desegregation?
- How did King propose to bring about social change?
- What is *passive resistance?*
- How did demonstrators behave at a lunch counter sit-in? Why did they behave this way?

Activities Leading Up to the Play Performance

During the six-week unit, the students were involved in a wide variety of learning activities, designed to help them participate knowledgeably in the improvisational drama session, the script writing, and also portray their character with an emotional understanding. During the preparation period, the students participated in some of the following activities (the list represents several years of activity with this particular unit):

- Read biographies of prominent figures in the cause for civil rights (King, Rosa Parks, Ghandi, Chief Justice Marshall, Mandela)
- Researched the conditions in society that precipitated the movement
- Read fiction that focused on the topic of racism in the South (*Gold Cadillac, The Road to Memphis, Mississippi Bridge, Ludie's Song*)
- Wrote poetry to honor King's birthday
- Wrote persuasive speeches with a particular issue in mind (for example, desegregation of housing, schools, restaurants) after viewing a documentary on King's life
- Viewed portions of the PBS series, *Eyes on the Prize*
- Researched fashion, music, fads, and so on, of the 1950s and 1960s to better portray their characters
- Improvised scenes of dramatic events in King's life
- Learned protest songs of the Civil Rights Movement: "We Shall Overcome," "We Shall Not Be Moved," "Ain't Gonna Let Nobody Turn Me 'Round"
- Created African masks in art class
- Participated in a dance movement piece depicting the capture, middle passage, and enslavement of Africans in the Colonies
- Participated in a scripted drama that combined scenes based on improvisational drama, narration, song, dance, and slides of King's activities

The Performance

The core of the King script was based on improvisational scenes developed in class. One is shown here as an example of how an improvised scene would look when scripted. The following is "Scene 7: Rich's Diner" from the play *His Name Was Martin*.

Scene 7: Rich's Diner

(Lights come up on the narrators at the microphones, and the stage is preset for the diner, with the actors frozen in place.)

NARRATOR: The bus was not the only place where blacks were segregated from whites. It happened in restaurants and lunch counters too.

NARRATOR: King tried to change this law. He staged sit-ins at lunch counters. At one of these demonstrations, he ran into some trouble.

(As the scene opens, people are seated at a lunch counter, eating and talking; the waitress is taking orders.)

WAITRESS: Y'all know what you want?

WHITE CUSTOMER 1: Yeh, I guess I'll have the Blue Plate Special.

WAITRESS: Y'all have a choice of mashed potatoes or fries. What'll it be?

WHITE CUSTOMER 2: Hey, Mabel! How 'bout some coffee over here?

WAITRESS: Just hold on . . . I'll be there in a minute. (Phone rings. Mabel looks exasperated, and walks over to answer it.) Mornin', Rich's Diner. No, he ain't here, and I don't expect him today. He called in sick and left me here all by myself. And I'm goin' crazy with customers. (pause) Yeah, I'll give him the message. Bye. (starts back to customer 1) Now, where were we . . . one blue plate . . . that's with . . . mashed potatoes or fries?

WHITE CUSTOMER 2: Can I have my coffee?

WHITE CUSTOMER 1: The fries, please, and I'll have coffee with that, too.

WHITE CUSTOMER 3: I'll have the same with mashed potatoes, oh, and an orange soda to drink.

WHITE CUSTOMER 4: Mabel, can I have my check please?

(Mabel crosses to other side of the counter, pours coffee and serves it to customer 2, then she prepares the check for customer 4. At the same time, four demonstrators enter the restaurant, including Martin Luther King, Jr. They sit down at the counter, pick up menus. The white customers begin to talk among themselves. Customers improvise conversation.)

WAITRESS: (turning around and noticing the black customers) Well, I never. . . . This is just what I need today (shaking her head, then going over to the demonstrators) Look . . . I don't want no trouble in here. You saw the sign. This is a Whites Only Lunchroom; no colored are allowed in here, so please . . . just leave . . . make it easy on yourselves.

KING: I'd like it to be easy, but from my experience the road to freedom is not an easy one. We're here to tell you that we have a right to eat at this lunch counter, and we'll sit here until we're served.

WAITRESS: And I'm here to tell you that this is an all-white lunch counter, and my customers don't want to eat with no coloreds. Y'all understand?

WHITE CUSTOMER 2: Yeah! We ain't gonna eat with no scumbag filth like you.

WHITE CUSTOMER 4: Just who do you think you are?

DEMONSTRATOR 1: We have the same right to eat as anybody else. I'd like a cup of coffee, please.

WAITRESS: You have no rights in this here establishment. I ain't servin' no colored, so *git out, or I'm calling the police!*

(Other customers join in. . . . Yeh!, get out. . . . No colored allowed. . . . I'm leaving. . . . etc.)

DEMONSTRATOR 2: We're not leaving. We simply want to be treated equally, like it says in the Constitution . . . "All men are created equal. . . ."

WAITRESS: (throwing up her hands) This is a waste of time. I'm calling the police.

(crosses to the telephone and dials) This is Mabel at Rich's Diner calling. I have a big problem here. A bunch of colored folk are sitting at my lunch counter and they refuse to leave. They say they're gonna sit here all day if needs be. Well, I sure as heck ain't gonna serve 'em, and they ain't gonna leave, so I sure would appreciate some help here. (pause) Okay, thank you. (crossing back over to the counter) Well, you heard me. The police are on the way, so if you don't want no trouble, y'all better git outta here real fast.

DEMONSTRATOR 3: We're not leaving. We have a right to be served. I'd like some coffee, please.

WHITE CUSTOMER 2: You wanna be served. Here! Have some coffee. (Customer throws a cup of coffee in the face of a demonstrator. The demonstrator doesn't move. Other customers are laughing and jeering at the demonstrators.)

(Police arrive on the scene.)

POLICEMAN 1: What's the trouble in here?

WAITRESS: You can see for yourself. These coloreds refuse to leave. They're just disrupting everything in here, causing me problems. . . . I don't have time for this.

POLICEMAN 2: Okay, let's move it. You heard the lady. You're not welcome here.

POLICEMAN 1: Get up now or you'll all be arrested for trespassing.

(No one moves. So, one by one, the police remove the demonstrators, who don't struggle but make their bodies stiff and difficult to move. Police improvise lines here: Let's go, come on, make it easy on yourself, move it, etc.)

(Lights fade to black.)

Assessment

Because I'm not training professional actors, I don't formally evaluate the students' performances during the play. I do notice, however, that all the students have developed a stage presence, have learned how to project, deliver a line clearly, and move around the stage with assurance. After the performance, I ask students to respond in writing to an open-ended question: "What did you learn from participating in the play production?" (See the section on oral and written response assessment in Chapter 6.)

While the class moves through the activities of this six-week project, the assessment is ongoing. For example, I might use my checklist to evaluate their work during improvisational sessions (see the section on assessment, Observation Checklist for Improvisation, in Chapter 3). When students read the biographies of King, Parks, and others, I use the "Guidelines for a Biography Response" (see Chapter 6) to evaluate their writing. When students are involved in the speech-writing activity, my evaluation includes an assessment of oral and written language as well as the historical content of the speech.

Speech writing, I've found, is a purposeful way for students to apply their research learning. During this civil rights unit, we watch several videotapes that have scenes of King, with his dramatic style of delivery, speaking to the crowds. After the videos, we discuss the attributes that made him an effective speaker and the main points of his speech. I ask students to write their own persuasive speeches to convince their audience of one of the following:

- Schools, restaurants, hotels, and so forth, need to be integrated.
- Housing laws need to be fair.
- Equal pay and job opportunity is needed for all.

I make my expectations clear, and explain the evaluation criteria to the students. When the speeches are delivered, I ask myself questions about the content and the delivery. If I incorporated my questions into a checklist, it might look something like the one in Figure 4–4.

Self-assessment is also an important part of the process. When the kids finish with any big project, they know I'll ask them to evaluate their work. For this assignment, I might ask them to respond to the following:

- What was the main point of your speech?
- List the arguments that you used to prove your point.
- When delivering your speech, what strategies did you use to capture the interest of the audience? (voice, gesture, facial expression, visuals, etc.)
- What did you learn from writing this speech?
- How would you rate your effort on this project?

Resources

Selected Professional Resources for Play Writing and Performance

Chapman, G. 1991. *Teaching Young Playwrights,* edited and developed by Lisa A. Barnett. Portsmouth, NH: Heinemann. This book outlines lessons that help students develop play-writing skills. Particularly helpful is Chapter 6, which discusses the basic play structure and guidelines to use when working with young playwrights.

Davis, J.H. & M.J. Evans. 1987. *Theatre, Children and Youth.* New Orleans: Anchorage Press. Davis and Evans focus on how to create quality theatre with children and youth. Chapter II provides definitions of prevalent theatrical styles and sets forth standards for production activity. Chapter VII ("Staging the Play") is particularly informative because it takes the reader through every step of the preparation for a performance.

Tarlington, C. & N. Michaels. 1995. *Building Plays.* Portsmouth, NH: Heinemann. Effective techniques for building plays with students are presented in this practical book. Chapter 2 outlines the stages in the play-building process, while Chapter 6 starts with the research stage and follows one project right up to the performance.

Speech Evaluation

Name_____   Date_____

	Outstanding	Good	Needs Improvement

Speech Writing

- Strong arguments were used, both factual and emotional _____ _____ _____

- The introduction captured the audience's attention _____ _____ _____

- The closing summarized the main point _____ _____ _____

- The historical content was accurate _____ _____ _____

- The language used engaged the listener's attention _____ _____ _____

The Delivery

- The student's voice was loud, clear, and had varied inflection _____ _____ _____

- The student employed gestures, eye contact, good posture _____ _____ _____

Effort _____ _____ _____

Figure 4–4. Speech Evaluation Checklist

The Civil Rights Movement and Martin Luther King, Jr.

Nonfiction

Adler, S. 1997. *Mandela*. New York: Writers and Readers Publishing.

Andryszewski, T. 1996. *The March on Washington: 1963 Gathering to Be Heard*. Brookfield, CT: Millbrook Press.

Authur, J. 1995. *The Story of Thurgood Marshall: Justice for All*. New York: Yearling.

Blackside (producer). 1986a. *Eyes on the Prize: America's Civil Rights Years. Episode 1: Awakenings (1954–1956)* [videotape]. Alexandria, VA: Public Broadcasting System.

Blackside (producer). 1986b. *Eyes on the Prize: America's Civil Rights Years. Episode 2: Fighting Back (1957–1962)* [videotape]. Alexandria, VA: Public Broadcasting System.

Blackside (producer). 1986c. *Eyes on the Prize: America's Civil Rights Years. Episode 3: Ain't Scared of Your Jails (1960–1961)* [videotape]. Alexandria, VA: Public Broadcasting System.

Cavan, S. 1993. *Thurgood Marshall and Equal Rights*. Brookfield, CT: Millbrook Press.

Celsi, T. 1991. *Rosa Parks and the Montgomery Bus Boycott*. Brookfield, CT: Millbrook Press.

———. 1991. *Jesse Jackson and Political Power*. Brookfield, CT: Millbrook Press.

Darby, J. 1990. *Martin Luther King, Jr.* Minneapolis: Lerner Publications.

Douglass, F. [1845] 1968. *Narrative of the Life of Frederick Douglass*. New York: Signet.

Elish, D. 1994. *James Meredith and School Desegregation*. Brookfield, CT: Millbrook Press.

Hakim, R. 1991. *Martin Luther King, Jr. and the March toward Freedom*. Brookfield, CT: Millbrook Press.

Haskins, J. 1992. *The Day Martin Luther King Was Shot*. New York: Scholastic.

———. 1992. *I Am Somebody! A Biography of Jesse Jackson*. Hillside, NJ: Enslow.

———. 1992. *One More River to Cross: The Stories of Twelve Black Americans*. New York: Scholastic.

———. 1992. *Thurgood Marshall: A Life for Justice*. New York: Henry Holt.

———. 1997. *Separate, but Not Equal: The Dream and the Struggle*. New York: Scholastic.

Hughes, L. 1994. "African Dance." In *The Dreamkeeper and Other Poems*. New York: Alfred A. Knopf.

Jakoubek, R.E. 1994. *James Farmer and the Freedom Rides*. Brookfield, CT: Millbrook Press.

Kent, D. 1993. *The Freedom Riders*. Chicago: Children's Press.

Lambert, K.K. 1993. *Martin Luther King, Jr.: Civil Rights Leader*. New York: Chelsea Juniors.

Levine, E. 1993. *Freedom's Children: Young Civil Rights Activists Tell Their Own Stories*. New York: Putnam.

McKissack, P. & F. McKissack. 1987. *The Civil Rights Movement in America from 1865 to the Present*. Chicago: Children's Press.

Milton, J. 1987. *Marching to Freedom: The Story of Martin Luther King, Jr.* New York: Dell Yearling.

O'Neill, L.A. 1994. *Little Rock: The Desegregation of Central High*. Brookfield, CT: Millbrook Press.

Parks, R., with Jim Haskins. 1992. *Rosa Parks: My Story*. New York: Dial.

Peck, I. 1968. *The Life and Words of Martin Luther King, Jr.* New York: Scholastic.

Schlessinger (producer). 1992. *Martin Luther King, Jr.: Civil Rights Leader: Black Americans of Achievement Video Collection* [videotape]. Bala Cynwyd, PA: Schlessinger Video Productions.

Fiction

Fennessey, S. 1996. *His Name Was Martin: A Play About Martin Luther King, Jr.* Carlisle, MA: Discovery Enterprises.

Herlihy, D. 1988. *Ludie's Song*. New York: Dial.

Moore, Y. 1991. *Freedom Songs*. New York: Orchard.

Springer, N. 1989. *They're All Named Wildfire*. New York: Atheneum.

Taylor, M.D. 1987a. *The Friendship*. New York: Dial.

———. 1987b. *The Gold Cadillac*. New York: Dial.

———. 1990. *Mississippi Bridge*. New York: Dial.

———. 1990. *The Road to Memphis*. New York: Dial.

Walter, M.P. 1982. *The Girl on the Outside*. New York: Lothrop, Lee & Shepard.

Wilkinson, B.S. 1987. *Not Separate, Not Equal*. New York: Harper & Row.

Publishers with Listings for Historical Drama

Anchorage Press
P.O. Box 8067
New Orleans, LA 70182
(504)283-8868

New Plays Inc.
P.O. Box 5074
Charlottesville, VA 22905
(804)979-2777

Discovery Enterprises Ltd.
31 Laurelwood Drive
Carlisle, MA 01741
1-800-729-1720

5

The Integration of Drama, Social Studies, and Language Arts

The play was fun because it was not like reading out of a text, we were actually walking in their shoes. It was so exciting that each morning I could hardly wait to get to school. I learned a lot about history, Harriet Tubman, Sojourner Truth, Frederick Douglass, what they said, felt, and did in their lives.

Amanda, age 10

A visitor stepping into my fifth grade classroom might see a variety of activities in drama, social studies, and language arts taking place simultaneously. These subjects interact naturally as students work in a series of class sessions to develop a project such as the Colonial Museum (described at the end of this chapter). In this instance, the visitor might see some students planning the layout of their visuals, cutting, pasting, and lettering. Others might be composing text for their display at the computers. A variety of books spread out on a table might engage the interest of several students as they research biographies for their colonial character portrayal. Another group might be discussing an improvisational scene with me in the drama circle, trying out ideas, then reflecting on whether or not they worked in the scene. Writing, reading, speaking, and listening are all being used purposefully to develop historical literacy and language arts skills. The integration happened naturally as students, enthusiastic about their class project, prepared for the opening of the museum. Without realizing it, they were developing crucial language arts skills.

Dramatic Arts Support the Development of Language Literacy

The use of the dramatic arts, more than any other strategy I've encountered, supports the development of language literacy. Here I've listed those behaviors that I've observed most often as the kids work on historical projects:

93

- *Fluency and self-confidence are enhanced.* The improvement of oral language is probably the most observable result of integrating creative drama and theatre practices into the social studies/language arts classroom. Because students are engaged in constant practice of oral language, progress is remarkable. Students are better able to think on their feet, becoming more fluent in debate or discussion. For some learners, having regular opportunities for participation in a safe classroom environment is enough to create the needed confidence to speak in front of others. They also learn to use their voices as an instrument, adjusting the volume, pitch, tempo, or quality to suit the character being portrayed.

- *Listening skills are developed.* In a play or improvisational drama, students must be active listeners to react to the line of another actor or to a specific cue. Their listening skills sharpen as they participate in a debate or a town meeting. They are induced to become critical listeners, assessing the opponents' arguments and coming up with alternative arguments, as well as the evidence to support them.

- *Improvisation functions as the fiction writer's oral rehearsal.* Donald Graves, in *Experiment with Fiction* (1989), makes the point that children compose fiction in play long before they write it, imagining themselves in a variety of roles, composing scenarios in their heads. The play acting (or dramatic improvisation) supplies the oral rehearsal for a piece of narrative writing, allowing a young writer to work on plot and invent characters, dialogue, and setting. Not only does drama play an important role in the prewriting stage, it also provides the motivation for writing, something that children constantly need. A student, for example, would be highly motivated to write, in script or narrative form, any one of the historical improvisations described in Chapter 3.

- *An understanding of literary elements is promoted.* After participating in the process of creating an improvisation or play, students are familiar with the basic elements of plot, character, setting, mood, and theme. During the preparation of a scene, as described in Chapter 3, the characters are discussed to determine what actions and dialogue reveal them to the audience. Students plan what scenery, props, and costumes indicate the setting. They recognize the importance of developing a plot structure that has conflict, with a beginning, middle, climax, and ending.

- *Reading is motivated.* As students prepare a readers theatre, an historical radio script, a video narration, a debate, a talk show, television broadcast, or any of the suggested activities in this chapter, they will need to read related material as part of the preparation. They will not only need, but also want to do it and be eager to do it. I have witnessed the enthusiasm. Often they regret that they can't find enough material to satisfy their needs. I keep a wide range of reading-level material on hand for historical reference, especially biographies, and have an active role in helping students locate and select appropriate readings. They also help each other by sharing resources and assisting those who might have difficulty with the reading. Students instinctively recognize that the more they know, the better able they are to participate successfully in the activities. I emphasize and model the importance of research to the creation of quality projects.

Oral and Written Language Activities with a Focus on History

There are a variety of language arts activities that actively involve students, helping them to become historically literate in ways that are exciting and motivating for them. The strategies presented in this chapter have students assuming the roles of reporters, radio announcers, voice-over narrators, debaters, public speakers, talk show hosts, museum guides, and storytellers. Each activity is described here with an example from American history.

Writing in Role

There are various types of writing in role, but they all have one thing in common; that is, children delight in using this technique. Assuming the character of another person as they write, I think, frees students from whatever preconceived notions they have about their own writing ability. They become another person from history. They are no longer a disinterested bystander because they have now stepped into the shoes of that person. Assuming the role of an ordinary or famous person, their writing takes the form of a letter, diary entry, memoir, autobiography, or newspaper eyewitness account or editorial. This strategy allows the students to share the feelings and ideas of the person being portrayed. They are, in fact, participating vicariously in the life of a person of the past. They are doing what Milton Meltzer (1993) aims to do when he writes history or biography, that is, establish a common bond with a person from the past. Gradually, students realize that these people were human, like themselves, not just words in a book. They are not giving a report about some dead person; instead, they *are* that person.

In the following example, students wrote diary entries from the point of view of a ten-year-old slave. To prepare for the writing, we read biographies of Harriet Tubman in literature group and listened to read-alouds from a variety of picture books on plantation life, and from slave diaries. Students then had some background information to help them assume the role of a young slave. From our various readings, they were also aware that most slaves could not read or write, and that teaching slaves to read and write was prohibited by law. So the activity began with the preface, "If slaves could read and write . . . ." The following is an example of a student writing in the role of a young female slave.

Excerpt from the Diary of the Slave Girl Fanny
by Katherine, age 10

I woke early this morning to the sound of the overseers horn. As I ran to the big house, I think 'bout the auction yesserday.* Me and my mama Chloe was sold to a Masta Robert Talda for a hundred dollas. The Masta poked and pulled at us. They lifted up our shirts to see if we got whip scars on our backs. . . . Mama says we is lucky because we was sold together. But mama works in the kitchen and I work as a servant for the Missus so we don't see each other much. . . . When I got in the big house, I go straight to the kitchen. There I get the tea and biscuits for the Missus. The platter is very heavy and I spill a tiny bit on the way. The Missus is lying in bed petting her cat. I curtsy and hand her tea. She slips me some biscuit and tells me to go braid her daughter Sarah's hair. The Masta is very mean, unlike the Missus. He cuss at me yesserday because I went into the kitchen to give mama some of the biscuit. . . . Slave meals are cornmeal and pork fat. There ain't never enough and I is always hungry. . . .

*(Note: The writer intentionally misspelled a number of words.)

In the second example of writing in role, the student assumes the role of an editor of a Southern newspaper during the Civil War. Before writing in role, students had read one of the following historical fiction books in literature group: *Charley Skedaddle* and *Who Comes with Canons?* by Patricia Beatty, and *Across Five Aprils*, by Irene Hunt.

Editorial from the Blue Mountain Herald, July 5, 1863
by Sam, age 10

The country is dead. Bloodshed of our neighbors and friends has killed it. The men of war have taken its spirit away with hate and death. No longer do they think about life. Now their minds are fixed on death upon their northern and southern neighbors. They have lit the country up into the flames of hate and denial. My friends, we have spit upon the flag, and no longer are we united. We are torn apart. The war must end.

Readers Theatre

Readers theatre is an effective yet simple way to stage a dramatic presentation. The presenters generally sit on stools and give a staged reading of prose or poetry. Movement is limited to facial expression, gestures, and body position. The voice is the chief instrument for the interpretation of the material. It is ideal for students in the middle and secondary grades who have had more experience using their voices effectively. Memorization is not necessary, but students need to analyze and discuss the text and become familiar with the context in which it was written. Preparation is crucial for students to interpret the readings with clarity, generating the necessary mood and emotion to the listeners. While preparing, students need to become familiar with the historical content and have the opportunity to practice their oral reading skills. Communicating the thematic content successfully to the audience becomes a focus and the motivation as the students rehearse the reading. It is important that the readings be appropriate for the ability of the performers. In a conference, I discuss possible choices with the students, and together we find readings that suit their talents and will be understood by the listeners.

Many types of literature are suitable for readers theatre. I have found that primary source documents such as letters, journals, and memoirs are particularly effective. Historical fiction provides rich characterizations. Selected poems or songs connected with narration are provocative, with descriptive language evoking images in the minds of the audience. It is possible to mix a variety of genres in one program with a single theme, or use one piece of literature performed by several readers. After selecting the material, the readers need to prepare an introduction and decide on the sequence. In one Civil War thematic program, students selected a variety of Civil War poems and wrote a narrative that took the listeners from the war's start through to the assassination of Lincoln. Folk music from the Civil War era was interspersed throughout the program. The poetry selections for this readers theatre were

"John Brown's Body" attributed to Charles Sprague Hall and Thomas Brigham Bishop

"Killed at Ford" by Henry Wadsworth Longfellow

"The Battle Hymn of the Republic" by Julia Ward Howe

"The College Colonel" by Herman Melville

"Frederick Douglass" by Langston Hughes

"Barbara Frietchie" by John Greenleaf Whittier

"O Captain! My Captain!" by Walt Whitman

A sampling of selected materials for thematic programs using the readers theatre format could be the following:

- Industrialization and Child Labor

  So Far From Home: the Diary of Mary Driscoll, an Irish Mill Girl, Lowell, Massachusetts 1847, by Barry Denenberg (fiction)

  The Lowell Mill Girls: Life in the Factory, edited by Joanne B. Weismann (primary documents)

  "'Bell Ballard' Goes to Work in a Cotton Mill." In *Child Labor in America*, edited by Julia H. Mofford

"Camella Teoli's Testimony Before Congress on Factory Conditions in the Textile Mills of Lawrence, Massachusetts." In *Child Labor in America*, edited by Julia H. Mofford

- Immigration
  Coming to America: A New Life in a New Land, edited by Katherine Emsden
  I Was Dreaming to Come to America: Memories from the Ellis Island Oral History Project, selected and illustrated by Veronica Lawlor
- Westward Movement
  Songs of the Wild West, commentary by Alan Axelrod and arrangements by Dan Fox
  Voices from the West: Life Along the Trail, edited by Katherine Emsden
- The Holocaust
  The Diary of Anne Frank, The Critical Edition, by David Barnouw and Gerrold Van Der Stoom
  The Endless Steppe, by Esther Hautzig
  The Hidden Children: The Secret Survivors of the Holocaust, by Jane Marks
  Images from the Holocaust: A Literature Anthology, by Jean E. Brown, Elaine C. Stephens, and Janet E. Rubin
  Night, by Elie Wiesel
  Rescue: The Story of How Gentiles Saved Jews in the Holocaust, by Milton Meltzer

Storytelling

In all of us, there's a bit of a storyteller. We tell our families and friends stories of everyday life, starting with "You won't believe what happened to me today . . ." and then go on to tell the story, enhancing it with dialogue and embellishing it to entertain our listeners. I use the art of storytelling in the social studies classroom, modeling for students how to use voice, gesture, and props to relate a story in a dramatic way. As the year progresses, I encourage the kids to try it for themselves. Stories of the following might be appropriate material for this purpose:

- a story of an historical event or person, selecting dramatic moments to capture the audience's interest (Example: the story of Cinque and the Amistad revolt)
- a folktale, myth, or legend that reveals information about a culture, traditions, or values of a society (Example: *Keepers of the Earth*, by Kaduto and Bruchac)
- a first- or secondhand account of a personal history (Examples that took place in my class: an African American teacher told stories of racist experiences in everyday life in a Southern town in the 1950s; a grandfather told

stories of his World War II experiences as an infantryman in Italy; a grand-mother related an account of what it was like working in a Rhode Island textile mill during the 1930s and after.)

Some students may not have the confidence or the skills to participate in this activity, which depends so heavily on oral language. Such students might choose to tell a story through movement, a song, or writing. It is also possible to work with a partner, sharing the responsibility for the delivery. I suggest to the kids that they use small index cards with listed key phrases that could be referred to if necessary during the telling of the story.

There is a wealth of suitable material available for storytelling. Well-written narratives, biographies, and memoirs are excellent choices. I look for material that has some dramatic interest, not only revealing historical information, but also capturing the attention of the listeners. I provide some guidance to students when they are choosing something other than a personal or family story. Magazines such as the *National Geographic* are also an excellent resource. While preparing for a unit on exploration, I once came across an article in this magazine on Magellan's voyage around the world. As soon as I read the article by Alan Villiers, I knew that it was great material for storytelling. The people, the settings, the problems encountered, and the writer's use of quotations from a journal by Antonio Pigafetta (the ship's chronicler) were incredibly vivid. It had all the realistically horrid details that would stir the imagination of any listener: mutinous captains, murder, shipwrecks, war, starvation, scurvy, and survival meals of rat stew and hide soup. I told the story in my words. It was a big hit with the students, inspiring them to read more about Magellan.

After making a selection, the storyteller should become familiar with the narrative so the telling seems natural and goes smoothly. The speaker's voice is also a consideration. Ideally, it should have a pleasant tone, variety in vocal expression, and clear diction, but this is not absolutely necessary for classroom purposes. One of the most fascinating storytellers I've encountered was an historian from the Smithsonian Institution. His voice had a matter-of-fact tone. He used little dramatic gesture, yet he was compelling because of the interesting anecdotes and descriptive details sprinkled throughout the tales of famous people caught up in the events of their time.

A small sampling of biographies that could be used either by the students or by the teacher as a basis for a storytelling is as follows:

Anne Hutchinson by Doris Anne Faber
Arctic Explorer: The Story of Matthew Henson by Jeri Ferris
Ben Franklin by Chris Looby
Bully for You Teddy Roosevelt by Jean Fritz
Clara Barton: Founder of the American Red Cross by Liz Sonneborn

Christopher Columbus Navigator to the New World by Isaac Asimov
Christopher Columbus on the Green Sea of Darkness by Gardner Soule
I, Christopher Columbus by Lisle Weil
The Incredible Journey of Lewis and Clark by Rhoda Blumberg
John Brown of Harper's Ferry by John Anthony Scott and Robert Allen Scott
The Life and Death of Crazy Horse by Russell Freedom
Mark Twain: A Writer's Life by Milton Meltzer
Quannah Parker by Len Hilts
Sacagawea: Indian Interpreter to Lewis and Clark by Marion Marsh Brown
Who Let Muddy Boots into the White House? A Story of Andrew Jackson by Robert
    Quackenbush
What's the Big Idea Ben Franklin? by Jean Fritz

Play Writing

Children's writing is often inspired by what they are currently reading. The girls who are reading mysteries want to write mysteries, and the boys who are reading fantasy tales create stories in that genre. After students participate in improvisational and scripted drama, I find that they are inspired to write plays. I encourage them to try out play writing, especially those students whose stories are filled with dialogue and little narrative. Very often the class talkers and socializers are naturals for this form of writing. They think and talk in dialogue: "He said . . . then she said . . ." and so on.

Play writing is not easily taught, nor easily learned. Having written plays myself, I struggle with the art form, but I'm learning through trial and error, through practice, and by using the experts as models. Students can do the same, using the scenes developed in class through improvisational drama as their models. I suggest starting out with one scene or two rather than an entire play. Several of the following ideas might help to get the writers successfully started:

- Students write a script for an historical improvisation already created in class. By doing this, they get a sense of how a scene develops, with a beginning, middle, climax, and end.
- Students create a script based on a scene from an historical fiction book. Here they have the advantage of having well-developed characters, plot, setting, and a conflict.
- Students create an original scene inspired by a character and situation in an historical fiction book.
- Students write a scene modeled after an event described in an autobiography, a biography, a diary, a journal newspaper, or testimony before a legislative hearing. (The type of personal narratives that Milton Meltzer uses in his books is excellent material for the basis of a dramatic scene.)

While students are writing their scripts, I conference with them often. During the prewriting and drafting stages, we discuss their main ideas for a scene, the characters, the setting, and how it will develop with a beginning, middle, and end. The questions I use in a play-writing conference are similar to the questions I use in a writer's conference for a narrative piece or the questions posed during the planning and revision stages of an improvisational drama (see Chapter 3 for questions).

Students usually have exciting ideas for a scene, but they're not quite sure how to develop them. During a conference, I try to help students identify what works, and then build on that. Through my questions, students realize that some situations and settings work well on stage while others are far more difficult to show to an audience. A battle scene from the Civil War may be exciting, but it's not practical to stage. But a scene before the battle, with several characters who reveal their fears as they anticipate the conflict, is more dramatic and manageable for staging purposes. Based on my observations of scenes created by young playwrights, I'd say that the most common problem is that they are finished in a flash. Before you can blink, the characters have said their lines, the scene ends, and a new scene begins, often in a different place and time. From the audience's point of view, they haven't had the chance to get to know the characters or care about them. The situation and the setting haven't been revealed to them. Sometimes, important details are left out that are needed for the audience to understand the plot.

Play writing is definitely hard work, but it is a worthwhile project for students because it promotes an understanding of human behavior while they practice and develop skills in the genre. I encourage students to employ a few general tactics when writing plays:

- Write a scene or two rather than an entire play.
- Write with a partner or small group.
- Seek conferences often with your teacher or peers.
- Try out the script with an oral reading.
- Get several class members to act out the scene while the playwrights watch it.
- Pick familiar situations and create characters that are near to your age. (Historical fiction is an excellent resource for this reason.)
- Keep the situations and characters believable by creating details and by motivating the characters' actions.

The following scene is a collaborative writing effort by a group of fifth graders. It is a script inspired by the book *The Endless Steppe,* by Esther Hautzig. The book is a true account of Esther Rudomin's life as a young Jewish girl exiled to Siberia during World War II. The students read and discussed the book as part of our literature-based study of history. After the reading, they chose to create a play for a group project. The play is not a scene from the book, but is inspired by events in the book and Esther's difficulties adjusting to the Russian school. The scene developed successfully because the situation was familiar (a classroom), they knew the main character well (Esther was discussed in literature group), and they had an established conflict (Esther was a Jew and a Polish immigrant in a Russian school).

Scene 1: A Classroom in Siberia

NARRATOR: This is a scene from a true story, *The Endless Steppe*. It's about a girl named Esther who is sent to Siberia with her family by the Russians during World War II. We enter her classroom late in the day.

(All students are writing with little noise.)

TEACHER: (in a rough voice) Time is up! Pencils down!

YURI: But I'm not finished yet.

TEACHER: (interrupting) I don't care! You had more than enough time to finish. Esther, collect all the papers now and bring them to me. (Esther collects all the papers and brings them to the teacher.) I have an announcement to make. There is to be a declamation contest in two months. You will choose a piece of writing and recite it in front of the judges. They will decide a winner. Here is a list of works from which you may make your selections. All students who would like to participate in the contest, raise your hands. (Seven students, including Esther, raise their hands and the teacher passes out papers to them.) Tell me your choices tomorrow. Remember, get plenty of exercise and rest because there will be a grammar test. For homework, do pages thirty-seven to thirty-nine in your grammar book. They will help you prepare for the test. Class dismissed.

(The students stand and bow to the teacher as she walks out. Some students follow her out, but two groups of children gather for conversation.)

SVETLANA: I think that Kutiusha will win, she wins everything.

ESTHER: How do you know, Svetlana? I might have a chance.

ANNA: You? Win? Ha! Ha! You can barely speak Russian, much less win a declamation contest.

SVETLANA: Stop it, Anna! You didn't even enter the contest, so you shouldn't be talking about who's winning it.

(Humiliated, Anna storms away, and the girls start to leave also.)

RITAN: Can you believe it? That Polish freak Esther entered the contest. Such nerve! How can she expect to win a Russian declamation contest?

RORUSKA: Of course she isn't. I'm going to win. She wouldn't stand a chance against me even if she was Russian.

YURI: I disagree! Even a Polish deportee could beat you, Roruska. I have it in the bag.

RITAN: Oh stop bragging you two. We'll see who wins on the day of the contest. (pause) Namely me.

(The boys all laugh as they exit the classroom.)

NARRATOR: The next day Esther confronted the teacher and told her that she had decided to recite Tatyana's Dream from *Eugene Onegin*. The teacher acted as if she didn't want Esther to enter, but Esther was very excited and charged home to tell her grandmother.

Scene 2: An auditorium in the school (several months later)

NARRATOR: Finally the day came. Esther entered the school auditorium early and went to the sign-in desk.
ESTHER: I'm here for the declamation contest. My name is Esther Rudomin.
MISS NIKITOVNA: (shuffling papers) I'm sorry. Your name is not on the sign-up sheet.
ESTHER: (alarmed) I'm sure I did. Could you look for my name again?
MISS NIKITOVNA: (looking through papers again) Ah, here you are. I see that you are reciting Tatyana's Dream. You may proceed.

(*Esther starts to go into the auditorium, but she is called back.*)

MISS NIKITOVNA: Wait a minute! You can't go on stage like that. Whatever made you think you could?
ESTHER: Like what?
MISS NIKITOVNA: Without your shoes, that's what!
ESTHER: (looks down at her dirty feet) I'm so sorry. I . . . I completely forgot to put my shoes on. Uh . . . wait a second. I'm sure, um . . . I know! I'll run back to my house and get some shoes.
MISS NIKITOVNA: You'll never make it on time. The contest starts too soon.
ESTHER: Please, just let me have a chance.
MISS NIKITOVNA: Well all right. I'll schedule your part near the end of the contest.
ESTHER: Oh. Thank you! (Esther dashes off the stage.)
NARRATOR: While Esther was having her shoe ordeal, the declamation contest had already started. We join it as a boy named Roruska is reciting.

(*Roruska is on stage mouthing the words. All eyes are trained on him, while a small group of students are talking.*)

RITAN: Did you see Esther earlier? She had no shoes on! She thought she could be in a contest without any shoes. She'd better hurry up, it'll be her turn soon. Not that it really matters. She couldn't do it anyway. It was good that Miss Nikitovna didn't let her in. She saved her from embarrassing herself. Don't you think so Svetlana?
SVETLANA: Well maybe Esther doesn't have any shoes, or can't afford them. Why do you always pick on her? She hasn't done anything to you. Just because she's from Poland doesn't mean that she's bad at everything. Leave her alone! You don't even know her.
YURI: Well, I don't even know why she entered the contest. She can't even speak Russian and she expects to win?
SVETLANA: Who cares? She's still trying, and besides, why do you care? She's not your friend.

(Esther dashes in and takes a seat next to Svetlana, panting madly.)

RORUSKA: (finishing the speech) . . . and that was Stalin's speech to the people. Thank you. (Everyone claps loudly as Roruska bows and walks off the stage.)
MISS NIKITOVNA: Our next speaker is Esther Rudomin, reciting Tatyana's Dream, by Pushkin.

(Esther walks on stage with slippers flopping loudly on her feet, still out of breath.)

ESTHER: (tiredly) An awesome dream Tatyana's dreaming . . .
NARRATOR: Esther recited her piece without fault. But she was too tired to even look at the audience. All the beauty of Tatyana's Dream was gone and her words seemed cold and lifeless. Even so, the one time she did look up, she saw an amazing sight. Her teacher was wearing a grudging smile, a look which Esther had never seen before. Even though a girl named Kutiusha won the contest, that look of respect was almost as good as winning.

(Curtain)

Slide or Videotape Presentations

When students exhibit a strong ability in visual–spatial intelligence, I capitalize on this by suggesting a slide or videotape presentation for an historical project. Whether working alone, with a partner, or in a small group, they need to plan the focus of their piece, discussing it with me in a conference.

One student in my class created a *slide presentation* on colonial architecture in Rhode Island. With an inexpensive automatic focus camera, he photographed houses representing various types of architectural design and materials in one city neighborhood. Once the slides were developed, he chose those that best illustrated the points made in his research report. Rather than write down the entire narration for his presentation, I suggested in a project conference that it might sound more natural if he wrote key words or phrases next to each slide number (for example, slide #4: gambrel roof) and then speak extemporaneously. The student agreed that he could do this, because, after preparing the slides, he knew his topic very well.

The creation of a *videotape production* is another way to nurture those students with visual acuity. Some families today have video cameras for home use, and audiovisual departments or libraries in schools will sometimes loan equipment to classrooms to be used under teacher supervision. For students who have access to a camera and the technical ability, this is an inviting way to present a project to an audience of their peers. Once again, I feel that conferencing during the planning stage of the production is necessary, especially if there is no editing equipment available. If shots are planned carefully, selecting only those scenes needed and in the desired order, the videotape can be used as is. It is tricky at times to concentrate on narrating and videotaping simultaneously, so I suggest to students to tape a voice-over narration separately, adding music if desired. In schools that are fortunate enough to have computerized editing equipment, there are many more options. Show titles, credits, music, and voice-overs can be easily added to the edited, finished product. Videotape production is especially useful for local history projects, interviews, or oral histories.

Capitalizing on New England's rich colonial history, two students in my class created a videotape on colonial farms. With transportation help from parents, they took shots of colonial farmhouses, barns, and stone walls, and visited an eighteenth-century, working farm museum to capture scenes of oxen at work, a sheep shearing, cow milking, farming tools, and so forth. One of the students appeared in some scenes, guiding the audience through the farm museum, interviewing the farmer and even some of the animals. It was a unique production, providing the rest of the class with abundant information on the subject that was unavailable elsewhere. The students had fun putting together the production, and both the videographers and the class learned a lot from this project.

The Radio Broadcast

Students living in the age of satellite communication and computer networks find it hard to believe that the radio, along with the newspaper, was once the fastest means of mass communication available. For topics such as the Depression of the 1930s and World War II, the radio is a natural medium for performance because it was one of the characteristics of the American culture at that time. Radio dramas of the 1930s were an entertaining diversion from the problems of the Depression, and during World War II, families gathered around the radio console to listen to on-the-spot reports from war-torn London or a battle site on a Pacific island.

For the learner who is hesitant about performing in a play or improvisation, radio broadcasting is a possible alternative. The actor is not seen, only heard, and projection isn't a problem with a microphone in use. Before I begin a radio project, I find that it's important for the kids to know something about the history of radio and how the medium works. One way to get a feel for radio broadcasting is to listen to original broadcasts. There are recorded collections that include the most popular radio dramas from radio's golden age ("The Lone Ranger and Tonto," "Sergeant Preston of the Yukon," etc.). Other recordings have World War II news reports of Edward R. Murrow and radio speeches of President Roosevelt and Prime Minister Churchill. By listening to a sampling of these and discussing them afterward, students realize that, unlike television or theatre, radio images are imagined, not seen. What works in a stage play won't work in a radio drama. The medium relies on the sound of the voice and sound effects, and is somewhat like storytelling. For the television broadcast (discussed later in this chapter), students had an immediate grasp of the medium and how it worked, but it takes longer to adjust to the concept of radio.

I recall how one class, talented and creative in drama circle, struggled with this project. The fact they could not be seen, only heard, was the source of frustration. Periodically, they would call me over to their group while working on a script for the news or a commercial to show me their latest idea. "Watch this, Ms. Fennessey. What do you think?" After observing, I would ask, "How will the audience see those props and those actions?" The answer was obvious, and so was their disappointment and frustration. Practicing with a tape recorder and microphone helped them focus on the vocal aspects of radio.

Once students have a feel for the medium, and have done the necessary research, they prepare a script. It could be news or drama, or a combination of both, with commercials (the sponsors). Sound effects really interest the students as they problem solve how to create a variety of sounds for the radio listener.

One such project that took place in my fifth grade class was connected with our study of World War II and the Holocaust. As part of a literature-based social studies curriculum, a group of students was reading Sonia Levitin's *Journey to America* and its sequel, *Silver Days*. In both books, there are scenes in which characters gather around the radio to hear the latest news of Hitler's movements and the war. Inspired by a scene in *Silver Days* in which the Platt family hears the news of the bombing of Pearl Harbor, the students created a radio show that captured the drama of that moment. The show included Big Band music, commercials, the news of the bombing, and an eyewitness being interviewed by a reporter on the scene in Hawaii. Through research and a visit to the school library, the students gathered the material to put together the show. They used actual newspaper accounts from the *New York Times* (front-page reprints) to write the news portion, borrowed a Big Band music recording from a grandparent, and wrote commercials for several products that were commonly advertised in the early 1940s. The eyewitness report was imagined from photos of the destruction found in history books. A second group, whose research topic was the Holocaust, broadcast in the Spring of 1945. This show included interviews with soldiers and officers who liberated the concentration camps, as well as stories of the survivors.

In the collaborative efforts, everyone handled several of the following roles: researcher, writer, news announcer, music announcer, actor or singer in commercials, news reporter, and as an eyewitness to the debacle. To present the project, students painted a large cardboard box to look like a console radio. One group taped the entire show on a cassette tape recorder, then placed the recorder inside the box with a "technician." The other group sat behind the radio and a fake wall to perform it "live from studio 4." The rest of the class gathered around the "console" and one of the kids mimed turning it on. We all listened to the historic broadcast with interest and great pleasure.

The Poetry–Drama Connection

Poetry has many uses in the social studies classroom. Children find its rhythm and imagery appealing. I've incorporated poetry in a variety of ways and have found these ideas to work:

- Students create their own poems on an historical subject.
- The teacher gives a dramatic reading of a poem (for example, "The Midnight Ride of Paul Revere," by Longfellow) to interest the students in a subject being introduced or to give inspiration for an improvisational drama.
- Students create a readers theatre performance (see this chapter) or a choral reading (see Chapter 4) of an historical poem.
- Students choreograph movement to a poem, first examining the mood and meaning of the poem to interpret its theme abstractly (for example, "African Dance," by Langston Hughes, as described in Chapter 4).
- Students write a rhythmic poem and set it to music.

As a teacher, I work to identify my students' talents, so at some point in the school year, I know who likes to write poetry. It is appealing to a broad range of students, especially those with a limited language ability and who exhibit difficulty composing narrative. Poetry is direct. It says a lot in a few words. Some of these students may not know how to spell the words or arrange them on the page, but their feelings are captured powerfully in several lines.

In a unit on World War II and the Holocaust, students in my class responded to the Johanna Reiss book, *The Upstairs Room*. As usual, they were given choices for their literature response. In this instance, they could respond in one of the following ways: Create a dramatic improvisation inspired by the book's content; write a poem that captures the main focus of the book; or write a first-person narrative in the form of a diary, assuming the role of a main character from the book. Out of a group of eight students, two chose to respond through poetry. One example is shown here:

The War in Holland

by Beth

The clouds of horror do not lift
from over a place called Holland
And the Jews that used to live there
will always be far from bliss.
For Hitler, a man so cruel and vain,
formed Nazi gangs that hated Jews.
and he gave Nazis the right to kill any Jew.
The Jews were afraid and they hid.
Years went by, and then it ended.

Everything ended.
The war had ended,
But the Jews still held pain.

In another project, which focused on the Harlem Renaissance and Langston Hughes, I read many of Hughes' poems aloud. Students were fascinated by their rhythmic quality. To "The Ballad of the Landlord," we created a clapping street game. Partners contributed different moves involving clapping, slapping, turning, and jumping while reciting the sing-song rhythms of the verses. Several weeks into the unit, we discovered that Hughes' birthday was that month. One of the kids suggested that we have a birthday party in his honor. I consented to help stage the event if everyone in the class created a present to honor Hughes. It was agreed that for a poet, the best present would be an original poem, a song, or a rap. So everyone set to work either alone, with a partner, or in a small group with the intention of presenting it at the party. Here is a poem composed by one of the fifth grade girls for the event:

Happy Birthday Langston Hughes

by Stacy

Happy Birthday Langston Hughes,
You're the poet that I would choose
In your life you had few rights,
Just because you weren't white.
It wasn't fair, no one cared,
Jim Crow laws were everywhere.
People just made such a fuss,
If you were black, to the back of the bus.
Three cheers for Langston, hip hooray,
He filled our lives with better days.
Langston, you were bound for glory,
Thanks for telling us the black people's story.

In the next example, the students wrote poems for one of the unit activities on civil rights and Martin Luther King, Jr. These students also participated in a full-length play performance for the school, entitled *His Name Was Martin*. At the end of the six-week unit, they had a solid knowledge base and strong feelings to convey in their poems. One student expressed his ideas in this way:

Martin Luther King, Jr.

by Brett

You saw the injustice
Even as a young man,

Your brothers and sisters
Mistreated throughout the land.

You were born a leader
And had a great dream
That all of God's children would
Finally be free.

Poetry with an historic theme, I find, is useful to arouse students' interest in a particular period of history, or as inspiration for a dramatic improvisation. There have been many powerful poems written on themes appropriate for social studies (war, human rights, Native Americans, frontier life, historical events, places, and people). An instance in which poetry was used as an inspiration for improvisational drama is described in Chapter 3 (Langston Hughes Experiences Jim Crowism). The poem, "The Merry-Go-Round," was used as a springboard for planning a scene and for a discussion of racial segregation. A sampling of poems that could be used for inspiration and motivation is the following:

"The Midnight Ride of Paul Revere" by Longfellow (American Revolution)
"Frederick Douglass" by Langston Hughes (slavery and abolitionism)
A Man's Body at an Auction, from "I Sing the Body Electric" by Walt Whitman (slavery)
The Runaway Slave, from "Song of Myself" by Walt Whitman (slavery/fugitive slave law)
"O Captain! My Captain!" by Walt Whitman (Civil War and Lincoln)
"Barbara Frietchie" by John Greenleaf Whittier (Civil War)
"Circling Back" by Gary Holthaus (westward movement, Native Americans)
"Behold, My Brothers" by Sitting Bull (Native Americans, the westward movement)
"Martin Luther King, Jr." by Gwendolyn Brooks (civil rights)

Staging a Debate

Once students have found that they have a voice, and they're no longer afraid to use it, there's no stopping them. They all have an opinion in class discussion, some quite emotional. They relish a formal or informal debate of a particular issue. Debating is an excellent format for teaching students that issues can be complex and have varying points of view. The challenge for me as a teacher is to get them to use logical arguments based on fact rather than only emotional ones. Ideally, there should be a balance of the two, but novice debaters often try to convince their audience to accept their point of view by appealing only to the emotions of the listeners.

In the example that follows, The Loyalists Versus the Patriots (a tea tax debate), a typical emotional argument on the Patriot's side might be: "The tea tax is a hardship on my family. I'm not a rich man. I can't afford to buy the expensive British tea and pay tax to a King in England who does nothing for us. It's always the same thing, tax the poor colonists to pay for the King's projects!" This emotional argument, although effective by giving a good solid reason for being against the tea tax, needs to be coupled with a more logical one to present to the audience some proof based on fact. Accordingly, the following logical argument might be offered by a debater taking the Patriot viewpoint: "We pay a tax on tea, which goes to the King of England. Yet we have no representation in the English Parliament, so we can't vote on any laws. Why should we pay tax to a government in which we have no representation?"

To strike a balance between logical and emotional proof, I allow one or two weeks for teams to research and prepare their arguments, conferring with each team often. I also work with the entire class to outline some of the basics of debating:

- the importance of understanding the question being debated
- the preparation of an opening statement in which a member of the team agrees or disagrees with the debate question
- the types of arguments used (logical and emotional)
- the rebuttal: listening to speakers on the other side and coming up with an opposing argument
- a closing statement in which each team summarizes the arguments for their side

After practicing the basics, I work with each team to help them locate the needed information and to discuss the arguments that they've prepared. I often assume the role of an opposing team member and state an argument. By doing this, the debaters have practice coming up with opposing arguments. Once the students have prepared their presentation, the debate can begin. I serve as the moderator to help move the debate along, rephrase a statement if needed, allow everyone to have a turn, and generally keep order if the arguments become heated.

For the topic cited here, the setting for the historical debate was Boston in 1773. Colonists were at odds over the tea tax imposed by the Parliament on all imported English tea. Patriots, not wanting to pay what they considered an unfair tax, were determined not to accept the cargo of English tea anchored in Boston's harbor. The Loyalists took an opposing stand and were willing to accept the tea and the tax that went with it. The question being debated was the following: Should the tea be unloaded from the ships in the Boston Harbor and the tax paid by the Colonists to the King of England?

When choosing teams, at first the majority want to defend the Patriot's position, but after studying the arguments for both sides, students realize that a strong case can be made for the Loyalist's point of view. Once teams have been formed, preparation begins. In this instance, because it was a reenactment of an actual meeting, the debaters wanted to role-play, choosing a character that was or might have been at the original meeting. To clarify their character's position in the community and their motivation for being at the meeting, debaters prepared a short statement about the person they were portraying. A character's point-of-view statement might look something like this:

> Edward Garrick (Patriot)
>
> I am a wigmaker and my shop is on King Street near the Custom House. More than two years ago, I witnessed the bloody massacre of innocent people by British soldiers. I'm tired of being pushed around by an English King and his redcoated soldiers. These taxes are just another way of bullying us and taking away our freedom. We pay them, but what do we have to show for it? We have no representation in Parliament. I see the rich Loyalists in my shop with their fancy clothes and jewelry, and I'm struggling to support my family. I work hard and barely get by. The taxes are too much of a burden. The tea tax is an unfair tax and I don't want those ships unloaded!

Being a good debater requires some linguistic talent, but I believe that everyone in the class can participate at their own ability level. If students have been regularly involved in creative drama and theatre activities, they have the confidence to assume a role in a debate. I encourage all to participate in debating because there is much to be gained from a learning experience of this type. Those that develop their skills in this area will eventually be able to do the following:

- make a point by speaking clearly and in simple, direct language
- research the topic and develop a set of arguments to support the case
- support arguments with a balance of both logical and emotional evidence
- listen critically to sort out important points made by the opponents and be ready to make a rebuttal that will attack their weakness
- be ready to defend the case from attack by the opposition with more evidence in addition to the original points made
- demonstrate gracious behavior toward the opponent and follow the rules set by the moderator

The Town Meeting

This role-playing activity is a particularly effective way to discuss social issues of the past and present. It is similar to the debate in that an issue is being discussed from several points of view. History is rich in ideas for town meeting topics, starting with the Puritans and continuing to the present time. A town meeting topic based on a current local issue has the benefit of timely newspaper articles, editorials, and letters to the editor, which reveal the facts surrounding the issue and present opinions of varying viewpoints.

I have taken many ideas for a town meeting subject from the local news section of the daily paper, or from historic accounts of controversial issues. Once the topic has been chosen, I have the students do background reading (I might provide photocopies of the articles or editorials that have appeared in the newspaper) and discuss the issues. In one real-life instance, our topic concerned the proposal of a large housing development in a wetlands area near the bay. The proposal was being met with opposition by environmental groups among others, and was being supported by a variety of special-interest groups who had the local economy in mind, as well as their own profit. As a class, we studied and discussed the facts surrounding the proposal. After everyone was familiar with the issues, I posed the following questions: "What types of people might be attending the town meeting? Who would be for the development? Against it? What would be their motives?" My questions continued, designed to provoke responses that covered a wide variety of citizenry. The list generated from this session looked something like this:

For the Housing Development
the developers
real estate attorneys
local merchants (hardware store, cleaners, drugstore, food market, gas station, car dealership, restaurant)
landscapers
home buyers
real estate agents
construction companies
housing contractors
retired citizens

Against the Housing Development
members of "Save the Bay" (environmental watchdog group)
fishermen
hotel owner
artists
some teachers
residents of the neighborhood
members of the Audubon Society and the Sierra Club
parents of school-age children
retired citizens

After completing the list, roles were assigned and groups began to prepare their statements and supporting arguments. During the preparation period, my job was to conference with each group to help them, through my questions, to generate arguments for or against the proposal. Next, I explained the procedure for a town meeting, pointing out that there would be five members of the council, with the head member presiding at the meeting. There would also be one or possibly two "stenographers," who would take notes on the important points made at the meeting. (It is helpful to outline a sequence of procedural steps for the meeting and leave it posted on an easel or board, visible to all the players.) Students then assumed the roles of the council members, and the remainder of the class became the citizens of the town. At the start of the meeting, the council head took attendance and announced the agenda for the meeting: an opportunity for citizens of the town to ask questions and voice an opinion about the proposed development. The head also made clear that everyone would have the opportunity to speak, but once someone had the floor, there could be no interruptions from other citizens.

After all speakers presented their points of view to the town council, the "stenographer" read the list of the arguments presented as a review before a vote was taken. The five members of the council then voted to approve or disapprove of the proposal. Other options might have been to continue discussion at another meeting or postpone voting while more studies were made concerning the effects of the development on plant, animal, and human life.

In follow-up discussion, students often express their frustration if their side loses, especially when there is strong evidence to support the rejection of a proposal. But the lesson learned is a good one: We don't always get what we want, and economic issues often have dominance over quality-of-life issues.

Oral History

It was the year of the fiftieth anniversary of the D-Day invasion when I first tried an oral history project with my class. That spring, almost every week, there were broadcasts interviewing American and German soldiers and French citizens who recalled their experiences at that time. Their stories were fascinating, as captivating as any good piece of theatre. So I thought to myself, why not find some war stories of our own?

We began by making a list of people who might know something about the war: the grandparent and great-grandparent generations (the most obvious for firsthand accounts), family relations, friends, neighbors, faculty and staff at the school, and veteran's organizations. Students asked the question, "Does it have to be a soldier? I don't know anyone that was in the war." The answer, of course, was, "No." I had hoped, in fact, that our histories would reflect the overwhelming influence that the war had on everyday life, which included civilian jobs and activities.

To model the process of an interview in an oral history project, I invited a war veteran to class. Before he came, I asked students to imagine that they were one of the reporters who had appeared on the television and to think about questions they might ask the veteran in an interview. Together we generated a list. We also discussed the fact that the questions needed to suit the subject being interviewed. Some questions that they would use to interview their relative or friend, I pointed out, would be different than the ones on our list.

During the interview session, we used a tape recorder. For the purpose of modeling, I asked the questions. I tried to show how important it was to be a good listener, to allow time for answers, and to ask good follow-up questions. After the interview, the students remarked that some questions from our initial list were not used. Instead, questions were generated from the responses given by the veteran. The next day, we listened to the tape for the purpose of finding the important parts and extracting quotations. I showed them that it was not necessary to transcribe the entire interview. For the next session, I presented students with a copy of my narration based on the interview.

Before the modeling sessions began, I sent a letter home explaining the project to parents and offering suggestions as to how they could be helpful. So, by the time we were to begin, most students already had someone in mind to interview. For the students who were having difficulty finding a subject (recent immigrants may not have family and friends nearby), I helped set up interviews with faculty and staff at the school. Students recorded interviews on tape, some via telephone, and several used video recorders. The result was a collection of stories that we ultimately bound in a book entitled, *The Untold Stories of World War II*. The writing took various forms: first- and third-person narratives and a question-and-answer format (an exact transcription of the tape).

The historical content of the book was amazingly broad, with detailed information about places, battles, air combat, soldiers' experiences, Jewish persecution, life on the home front, and the emotional effects of war. The historical understandings that were revealed through the writings were as follows:

- There are a wide variety of jobs in the armed services. (Our subjects included paratroopers, an airplane mechanic, a tank commander, an engineer, a radio operator in the Signal Corp, a radar expert, an air spotter, a crew chief in the Air Corp, an infantry soldier, a field medic, a reconnaissance pilot, a bomb squadron pilot, an intelligence officer, a typist, and an Army nurse.)
- Nonmilitary jobs were important to the war effort. (Our subjects included a boat builder, a female welder in a shipyard, a wire cable factory worker, a worker in a factory that made generators, and a member of the Coast Guard auxiliary.)
- For people who lived in countries invaded by Hitler's army, life changed drastically. (Our subjects included an Italian immigrant living in Italy during the war and the wife of a French resistance spy).
- Jews were captured and sent to work or death camps as part of Hitler's master

plan to exterminate Jews. (Our subjects included a German Jew hidden by sympathizers and a Polish Jew sent to Siberia.)

- The war was widespread, involving many countries in the world. We marked locations on a world map that were the setting for the oral histories. (The places included Berlin and Mannheim, Germany; Bologna, Italy; Groesbeek, Holland; Nagasaki, Japan; New Guinea; Curmotola and Calcutta, India; Burma; the Bay of Bengal; Egypt; China; the Philippines; England; France; Leyte Gulf; Rhode Island; and Pearl Harbor.)
- The war affected the lives of the average citizen in the United States. (Our subjects told stories of food rationing and coupon books; shortages of gasoline, meat, and other items; blackouts; war bonds; civil defense groups; victory gardens; and collecting newspapers, foil, and tin.)
- The war had an emotional effect on those involved. (Our subjects included soldiers who were lonely, frightened, angry, or disturbed after the war, and wives who were worried).

The following are excerpts from the oral histories recorded by the fifth grade students:

(An excerpt from an interview with a reconnaissance pilot, by Carter)

My grandfather lived first in tents, then in huts on the island of Leyte in the Philippines. They had simple food and not much entertainment. In their free time, they played cards, talked and rested a lot. The missions were very stressful since there was always the fear that a Japanese fighter plane would appear out of nowhere, especially during a landing or takeoff when they were flying very slowly. He flew alone in his plane, but always in a group of reconnaissance aircraft. His work consisted of keeping the plane level while flying over reconnaissance sites and working the camera controls so that the camera would get the entire picture for the ground that was being observed: railroads, bridges, camps, factories, artillery sites before and after attacks by U.S. bombers.

(An excerpt from an interview with a German Jew, by Phoebe)

When World War II started in September of 1939, I was in the capital city of Germany, Berlin. I was steadily on the run for my life because I am Jewish, and as everybody knows, the fascists tried to kill all the Jews. I tried to hide, which I did very successfully, but unfortunately, my family did not. I was with a group that was in opposition to the fascists and I lived there with them in the underground. Food was scarce, and there was always the fear everyday that I could have been caught by the fascists and we know what would have happened if I had been caught.

(An excerpt from an interview with a Polish Jew, by Elyssa)

When the war began, people were shot in the street, their houses burned down, just because they were Jewish. When his family went from Poland to Russia, they were taken from their beds, able to take no belongings, no money, nothing, and were taken on a train for four weeks with no food, and were taken to live in the woods in Siberia. They worked all day for an extremely watery bowl of soup at 4:00 AM and a single piece of bread later. They lived that way for two and a half years. Both his mother and father died of starvation.

(An excerpt from an interview with his Italian grandmother, by Sal)

I was born in Carasa, Italy and I was 21 years old during the war. The Germans came to my house in the middle of the night and took our matresses and sheets and went to the first floor to sleep. There was a total of five Germans living in the house with our family. We were all very scared because the Germans would make the Italian women cook and then bring food to the front line where the war was happening. The town people reacted very scared because the people were afraid that the Americans would bomb the town. As the war grew closer and closer to my town, the Americans started bombing closer and closer. We lived in a two story house and my father slept on the second floor. One day when the bombs started falling, one landed so close to my house that the sewer cap flew in the air and went right through the roof and on my father's bed.

This project gave the students a detailed look at the past as they heard the personal histories of soldiers, refugees, prisoners, and civilians. It impressed on them and me how much the war affected people's lives, and gave real meaning to the words *world war*. For all of us, there was a deep understanding that history is created by real-life people. We had met them and heard their stories.

The Living Timeline

The inspiration for this activity came from watching an actor do a character portrayal of Amelia Earhart at a social studies conference. Dressed in costume, she made this person's life come alive as she told about Earhart's adventures in flying. Initially, I thought about having her perform for my students, but we didn't have the funds for a school visit. It was late in the school year, and we'd spent every bit of money allotted for such things. With my class involved in creative drama and theatre activities since September, I figured that they could create their own character portrayals.

One way to look at history, I thought, was through the people who made it. I came up with a core list of famous men and women of the twentieth century, a variety of personages in many fields. Other names were suggested by the students and were added to the list. Assuming the role of a person, the student was to create a short autobiography (performed as a one- to two-minute monologue), emphasizing the event, discovery, or type of work for which the person became famous. I told students that we would be creating a *Living Timeline*. Actors would be placed on the timeline in chronological order to help everyone understand sequence and relationships. A date that represented a significant event in the life of the character needed to be selected and the importance of it explained in the monologue. Students were eager to wear costumes, so we checked out a book on period costumes from the school library to look at clothing styles of the different decades in the twentieth century. The preparation then began with a selection from a list of the following male and female characters:

Thomas Edison, inventor
Woodrow Wilson, president
Albert Einstein, scientist
Franklin D. Roosevelt, president
Winston Churchill, prime minister
Martin Luther King, Jr., civil rights leader
John F. Kennedy, president
Henry Ford, business leader
Walt Disney, filmmaker
Robert Goddard, scientist
Langston Hughes, poet
Louis Armstrong, musician
Thurgood Marshall, justice
Jesse Owens, Olympian
Duke Ellington, musician
Babe Ruth, baseball player
John Glenn, astronaut
Charles Lindbergh, aviator
Richard Nixon, president
George Gershwin, musician
Matthew Henson, explorer
Susan B. Anthony, women's rights activist
Frances Perkins, cabinet member
Bessie Smith, singer
Eleanor Roosevelt, stateswoman
Babe Didrikson, Olympian
Amelia Earhart, aviator
Mary McLeod Bethune, educator
Georgia O'Keeffe, artist
Sally Ride, astronaut
Dorothea Lange, photographer
Rosalyn Carter, stateswoman
Isadora Duncan, dancer

Rachel Carson, environmentalist
Margaret Mead, anthropologist
Rosa Parks, civil rights activist
Mary Harris Jones, labor organizer
Christa McAuliffe, astronaut
Maya Angelou, poet
Sandra Day O'Connor, justice
Shirley Chisholm, politician
Marian Anderson, opera singer
Barbara Jordan, congresswoman
Marjory Stoneman Douglas, environmentalist

After the person was chosen, the next step was to research and write a monologue. I suggested encyclopedias for capsule versions and biographies as a source of detail for quotations and photographs. To help the students with the writing, I presented a written monologue during a minilesson. Stressing the importance of keeping within the one- to two-minute time frame, I showed them how to feature the highlights of the person's life. I also pointed out that writing for an oral performance was different than writing for reading. Sentences can be shorter and simpler. The style can be more personal, more like conversation. The following monologue was used in the minilesson:

> Hi, my name is Marjory Stoneman Douglas. I was born in Taunton, Massachusetts, in a big old house. When I was young, I loved going to the attic to read. I guess that's why I studied literature and writing at college. After I finished at Wellesley College, I tried different jobs, but I ended up in Miami. That's where my father lived. He was editor of the *Miami Herald*. If you've visited Miami, you know that it's a huge place—over three million people. But, when I went there in 1915, there were only about five thousand. We had this governor then who dreamed about developing Florida, so he came up with the crazy idea of draining the Everglades. Can you imagine? That beautiful place, filled with giant cypress, panthers, all kinds of birds. I was shocked! Right then I became determined that it wouldn't happen. So I spent the rest of my life trying to save this unbelievably beautiful place. I used my writing talent to convince people not to drain the Everglades. I won that battle, but there were others. I chose the year 1947 as an important one for me. That was the year that my book, *Everglades, River of Grass*, was published. And that's the year that the Everglades finally became a National Park. I've spent my life trying to educate people about the environment. I hope you take an interest in yours—join a local group and speak out. Notice the life around you, and make a difference in the world.

For the event, every actor needed a date displayed on their person. Some students had them pinned, others on a string around their necks, on hats, purses, sandwich boards, and placards. The performance was divided in two parts, performed chronologically, with an intermission for refreshments. Each half ran about twenty to twenty-five minutes. I took photos of each character in performance. The following week, we created a timeline with the photos to hang on the wall, documenting the project.

A Television Broadcast (talk show, newscast)

Students who have been brought up with television are familiar with the medium and feel comfortable with it. They view it as entertainment. When I use a television broadcast format as a learning medium, I first try to impress on students the importance of planning and teamwork. What we see when we turn on the television, I tell them, is the result of research, purposeful writing, rehearsal, and technical coordination.

I have used this activity as a culmination of a unit, a unique way of presenting research, or a literature group project. It is appropriate for a small or large group of students. It can involve more students by employing a technical crew (camerapersons, floor director, and people in charge of props, sound, and visuals). To make it historically believable, actors need to be dressed in appropriate period costume, just enough to suggest a time.

The subject of a talk show or a newscast can feature any historical event or theme. Characters can be real historical figures or be selected from historical fiction. We've incorporated both into productions and it works just fine. Students know the real from the fictional, and the historical information remains the same.

In the *talk show format*, the host interacts with the guests, and the guests interact with each other. At times, I've used co-hosts to increase the flow of questions that are necessary to keep the talk moving. Any number of historical people, both real and fictional, can be assembled to discuss a topic. During the planning conference, I try to suggest characters with a wide range of perspectives to create interest. In one instance, students created a talk show based on an idea from an historical fiction book set during and after the American Revolution (*Jump Ship to Freedom*, Collier & Collier). This book, and others, had been read as part of our literature-based social studies curriculum. Consequently, the students already had an intimate knowledge of the characters. At one point in the novel, the main character, the slave Dan Arabus, finds himself at the Constitutional Convention in Philadelphia. At the convention, the issue of slavery was a controversial topic. The students used this idea for a talk show focus: Should slaves be guaranteed their freedom in the Constitution? A guest list for the show was created by selecting people from books we'd read in class. The students considered gender and point of view when making the selections. The list looked like this:

Daniel Arabus, slave (*Jump Ship to Freedom*)

Nathaniel Bowditch, navigator and former indentured servant (*Carry On Mr. Bowditch*)

Ben Franklin, delegate to the convention and inventor (*Shh! We're Writing the Constitution*)

Joseph Plumb Martin, soldier (*A Young Patriot: The American Revolution as Experienced by One Boy*)

Deborah Sampson, soldier and lecturer (*The Secret Soldier: The Story of Deborah Sampson*)

Abigail Adams, women's rights activist and wife of John Adams (*They Led the Way: 14 American Women; Abigail Adams: Witness to a Revolution*)

For some characters, like Arabus, the point of view was clear. For others, the actors needed to speculate what their position on the issue might be, based on their knowledge of the person's life. Questions were prepared by the hosts, and each guest wrote a point-of-view statement to which they could add additional comments to support their position. After the show was videotaped, the class enjoyed seeing their work on television, and participated in a discussion and assessment of the project.

In a *television newscast*, the show content is more varied. There are news anchors who read the local, national, and world news; on-the-scene reports; interviews; weather; sports and entertainment news; and commercials. To acquaint students with a news show format, I have them watch the local news broadcast, noting the content of the show. After the subject of the newscast is decided (usually what is currently being studied in history), students choose a role and begin their research to prepare for their presentation. During the planning stage, I conference with students to discuss problems particular to an historical broadcast and to stress the importance of historical accuracy. We brainstorm a list of resources that could be helpful in their research: history books, a timeline book, encyclopedias, an atlas, and primary documents.

In one fifth grade class, we researched World War II, investigating it through a variety of strategies. Literature was one of the ways we were able to explore the topic in-depth and from multiple perspectives. Three historical fiction books that students had read (*The Endless Steppe, Snow Treasure, Journey to America*) were used as the source of ideas for the newscasts. The historical information revealed through the novels and the setting provided much of the content for the shows. The *Endless Steppe* group, for example, created SSN (Siberian Steppe News), broadcasting in November of 1942 from Rubtsovsk, Soviet Union. World and national news items for the show were found in history books that provided a chronology of the war. Local news items reflected events in the novel. Each news show

Figure 5–1. Students Rehearsing an Evening News Show

had a different broadcast date, thus covering more of the war. The *Journey to America* group broadcast from Zurich, Switzerland, on November 12, 1938, and the *Snow Treasure* group chose April 1940 in Riswyk, Norway. News items for each show were different. For the Swiss reporters, Kristallnacht was the feature story. Russian reporters opened with a story on a major counterattack by the Red Army, and the Norwegians headlined with the German invasion of Copenhagen.

The texts also inspired the commercials and weather reports. In Switzerland, the commercials were for cheese, chocolate, a pawn shop, and a ski resort. The Siberian news show featured commercials from the *baracholka* (a marketplace), using Russian words such as *sapogy* (boots) to advertise the products. The Norwegian group's weather segment included a marine forecast for the fjords, skiing, and ice-skating conditions.

Each newscast was unique in historical content, providing reports, interviews, and eyewitness accounts, and one even included an editorial on the problems of refugees. To create a more believable newscast, students found it necessary to research the country from which the news would be broadcast. War events, geography, culture, and climate were a few of the areas studied.

Once students had prepared the scripts for the broadcast, I set aside time to plan the show's sequence and location changes, rehearse their readings, and practice using visuals. I encouraged students to aim for smooth transitions. They sometimes tried to include too many short pieces, which made the show's rhythm choppy. A complete run-through before taping solved some of the transition problems.

From participating in either a talk show or a newscast, students have the opportunity for growth in language arts, social studies, research skills, and social development. They gain a better understanding of the genre of broadcast news by participating in the hands-on event, and while in production, they're involved in critical thinking, decision making, and exercising judgment as to the show's content.

Public Speaking

Public speaking provides yet another opportunity for students to experience history. During the past, speeches to inform, protest, persuade, honor, or commemorate have been made by famous individuals on many occasions. Lincoln's Gettysburg address, Sojourner Truth's "Ain't I A Woman" speech, and Martin Luther King's "I Have a Dream" speech are some of the obvious examples, but there are many more choices for oratory purposes. Often, the entire text of the speech or excerpts are printed in historical or primary document books. Students can use these speeches to learn more about the famous individual. For an exercise in oral interpretation, I have students read or recite sections of a speech. I've found this particularly helpful to some students as a confidence builder. I work individually with them to improve delivery, stressing articulation, correct pronunciation, inflection, emphasis, pause, and rhythm. As self-assurance increases, they are prompted to add gestures and increase projection. Once a famous speech (or an excerpt) has been prepared, an audience is needed. I've incorporated famous orations into play performances, readers theatre, Living Timelines, and classroom museums. This provides an appropriate forum for the presentation of a speech. I find it more workable if only a handful of children are involved in this activity, rather than the entire class.

Another way to utilize public speaking in the social studies classroom is to have students write their own speech, assuming the role of a person from the past. They might prepare a speech for a special occasion, for example, a eulogy for a famous individual. Other ideas might be an introduction of a famous person, a dedication of a monument or building, a birthday tribute, or a presentation of an award. One student in my class read a biography of Phyllis Wheatley and wanted to create a speech about her. Although Wheatley was not an orator, she did do some public recitations of her poetry. In a writer's conference with the student, I suggested that she imagine a situation in which Wheatley was being given an award. Using the information that she had gathered in research and the reading of the biography, the student decided that she would write the speech from the perspective of a presenter and award Wheatley the Pulitzer Prize. (The student was certain that Wheatley would get it if she were alive today.)

In addition to practicing research skills, the students who are engaged in speech-writing activities discover that speech writing has its own characteristics unique to writing-to-be-heard rather than writing-to-be-read. The characteristics are the following:

The speech purpose needs to be clear to the audience.
The sequence should be organized and logical, to make it easier for the listener.
Each idea needs to be developed and appropriate examples given.
The style should be personal and direct, using short simple sentences, because the audience only hears the speech once.

When the students are ready to deliver the speeches to an audience, they must choose how to do it: recite from memory, read from a script, or speak extemporaneously, referring to notes or cards with quotations and examples. After they choose the appropriate mode, I encourage them to have eye contact with the audience and speak energetically, using gestures and facial expressions. I emphasize these factors because the oral delivery determines the success of a public speaker.

In the Spotlight: A Colonial Museum

The inspiration for the classroom museum came originally from the activity *Artifacts,* described in Chapter 2. When the kids showed their artifacts to the class, I thought that this was an exciting way to involve them in teaching others, and, given a topic focus, it could be done on a much larger scale, such as a museum exhibit. Later on that year, during a study of colonial life in America, we immersed ourselves in a variety of activities to understand how Colonists worked and played. Creating crafts, playing colonial games, participating in a Colonial classroom simulation, and making bread and homemade butter were some examples. The museum gradually emerged from these activities, the students' accumulated research, and replications of art and artifacts created in class.

A museum is an exciting and challenging way to present research, and it was my main reason for using it as a culminating project. It integrated the arts, social studies, and language arts in one setting. Most importantly, the preparation for the exhibits capitalized on the intelligences of each child.

Throughout the unit on colonial life, the kids researched a specific topic with the purpose of becoming an expert on that subject. In addition, there were general topics that they all studied, providing a common knowledge base for everyone in the class. When it came time to plan and prepare the museum exhibits, much of the research had already been done. I then grouped the kids to create the exhibits. For example, individual topics such as Colonial architecture, the kitchen, weaving, and candle and soap making were grouped in an exhibit titled *Colonial Home Life*. After all the students were organized in an exhibit group, we discussed the following questions:

- What is the purpose of the museum?
- What are various ways to create exhibits?
- Why are captions and explanatory statements important?

The answer to the first question seemed to be evident to most students because they had had a number of visits to local museums during their past five years in schools. The second question was less obvious, and I needed to ask a number of follow-up questions to generate their thinking about exhibit possibilities. Fortunately, we live in an area with access to excellent museums that use interactive and immersion strategies to educate and excite museumgoers. After questioning the students about the strategies that museums use to create exhibits, we came up with a list of possible devices for making our own museum. They were the following:

- artifacts (real or replicas)
- replications of arts and crafts (weaving, woodworking, stenciling, etc.)
- dioramas
- pictures, photos
- charts, diagrams, maps, timelines
- copies of primary source documents
- audiovisual aids (videotape, slides, tape recorders)
- live demonstrations
- music
- dance
- simulations
- lectures
- role playing in period costume

The third question stimulated the group to think about organizing and presenting the materials under each unifying topic, such as Colonial Home Life. They had to decide what information needed to be displayed on cards and poster boards to help the audience understand the exhibit. They also had to plan the use of space, exhibiting their materials clearly, logically, and artistically.

After the discussion, I allowed the kids time to plan as a group, create visuals, write the text for the exhibit signs, gather or make artifact replicas, and mount photos or photocopies of primary documents. I set deadlines to help the cooperative groups work productively. Because the students had been involved in individual research and classroom learning on the topic during the previous four to six weeks, they had sufficient information to create an effective exhibit to speak knowledgeably as tour guides during the event. Members of each group helped each other according to their talents. The writers worked on the text for the exhibit. Those who were artistically talented created graphics, replicas, and historical maps. As they worked, I interacted with groups, checking progress and helping students choose effective devices to reveal the ideas being presented in the exhibit. I roamed from group to group, conferencing as needed and assessing group progress and cooperation.

A Colonial museum created by my fifth graders had six main exhibits. They were the following:

Exhibit	Devices Used
Home Life (clothing, kitchen, products, crafts)	artifacts, demonstrations, models, slides
On the Farm (tools, crops, animals)	diorama, charts, artifacts, videotape, pictures
Arts and Crafts (tinsmith, potter, wigmaker, printer)	demonstrations, artifact replicas, photocopies
Toys and Amusements	demonstration of games, toys, and minuet; replicas, pictures, music, photocopies
Transportation and Trade (ships, ship building, triangle slave trade)	slide/lecture, diagrams, photocopies, charts, tape-recorded slave stories, models
Colonial Schools	artifact replicas, school-day simulation, interactive learning in the "school house"

As the museum set-up day drew closer, we worked out a floor plan for the entire museum on chart paper. Consideration was given to traffic flow, safety for certain demonstrations (for example, candle dipping), and sufficient space for the Colonial classroom simulation and the minuet demonstration. A schedule of museum *Special Events* was posted, in the classroom and out in the hall, that included time listings for the simulated Colonial school, the minuet, Colonial games, and demonstrations of toys and candle dipping.

We used painted refrigerator boxes, cut and stretched out to create wall panels down the center of the classroom. Desks, covered with cloths, were placed in front of the panels on both sides to display artifacts and signs. Special areas were set up for demonstrations, dancing, and the Colonial classroom.

Figure 5–2. The Colonial Museum Is Set Up and Waiting for Visitors

Parents, alerted to our project in a letter home, were extremely helpful by providing the necessary support for gathering museum materials as well as costume pieces that would give a suggestion of Colonial times.

On the day the museum opened, classes arrived at their scheduled time and toured the museum. The interactive exhibits were the big hits. Younger students played with all the Colonial toys and sat in the simulated classroom trying on the dunce hat. Older students tried their hands at weaving, spinning, candle dipping, or pressing the tape deck to listen to a slave's account of a journey on a slave ship. Special events, such as the Colonial classroom drama and the demonstration of the minuet, were especially appealing to the parents.

Students, when asked to write about their museum experience afterward, were enthusiastic in their assessment. They felt that they knew their subject well, had learned their classmates' topics also, and were able to confidently teach others about Colonial life.

Assessment for the Museum Projects

When evaluating the museum projects, I consider the preparation process as well as the final product. Ongoing assessment takes place when I observe and conference with students as they create their exhibits. Directions and requirements are

Figure 5–3. Emeline Lectures at the Colonial Museum. RIC Office of News & Public Relations, Gordon Rowley, Photographer

clearly spelled out during the planning stages, so as I conference, I refer back to the planning sheet and ask questions such as, "Are your pictures arranged logically?" and "Do you have an explanation to go with each picture or artifact?" When the exhibits are presented, I consider the historical content and how it was presented visually. Evaluation might be done by using a checklist, such as the sample in Figure 5-4.

Resources

Selected Professional Resources

Ayres, J. & J. Miller. 1983. *Effective Public Speaking.* Dubuque, IA: Wm. C. Brown. This is a comprehensive text on public speaking, with chapters on speech writing in general and two excellent chapters that focus specifically on constructing a persuasive speech.

Bosma, B. 1992. *Fairy Tales, Fables, Legends, and Myths: Using Folk Literature in Your Classroom.* New York: Teachers College Press. This book contains a very helpful annotated

Museum Project Evaluation Checklist

*Name*_____ *Title of Project*_____*Date*_____

	Excellent	Good	Fair	Not Evident
The Content:				
1. shows evidence of research	_____	_____	_____	_____
2. clearly informs the viewer of the topic with an introduction and explanation of visuals	_____	_____	_____	_____
The Visuals:				
1. show planning and organization in the layout	_____	_____	_____	_____
2. show originality and inventiveness	_____	_____	_____	_____
3. are displayed clearly and artistically	_____	_____	_____	_____
4. are appropriate choices for the topic	_____	_____	_____	_____
Group Cooperation:	_____	_____	_____	_____
Effort:	_____	_____	_____	_____

Devices used in the exhibit: (circle)

pictures   photos   diorama   slides   timeline   maps   models

charts   diagrams   artifacts   videos   taped voices   music   dance

role playing   costume   simulation   replicas of primary source documents

live demonstration   other_____

Comments: _____

Figure 5–4. Museum Project Evaluation Checklist

guide to recommended folk literature. Chapter 6 outlines creative activities with folk literature, including storytelling and readers theatre.

Chapman, G. 1991. (Edited and developed by Lisa A. Barnett) *Teaching Young Playwrights.* Portsmouth, NH: Heinemann. This book outlines lessons that help students develop play-writing skills. Particularly helpful is Chapter 6, which discusses the basic play structure and guidelines to use when working with young playwrights.

Edinger, M. & S. Fins. 1998. *Far Away and Long Ago: Young Historians in the Classroom.* York, ME: Stenhouse. Each chapter has detailed descriptions on the development of a particular social studies unit. Chapter 3 gives a step-by-step account of one oral history project.

Graves, D. 1989. *Experiment with Fiction.* Portsmouth, NH: Heinemann. Graves' book emphasizes that both the teacher and the student need to experiment with writing to become better at it, that reading and writing integrate naturally, and that minilessons are crucial to the success of teaching writing.

Meltzer, M. 1993. "Voices from the Past." In *Journeying: Children Responding to Literature,* eds. K Holland, R. Hungerford, & S. Ernst, 27–30. Portsmouth, NH: Heinemann. Meltzer and other well-known authors make the case for using literature in the social studies classroom to make history more stimulating and dramatic for students. Chapters 10 through 13 take us into the classroom with in-depth examples of teachers who employ a literature-based social studies curriculum. The annotated bibliography of trade books is organized thematically and has many excellent titles.

Selwyn, D. 1993. *Living History in the Classroom: Integrative Arts Activities for Making Social Studies Meaningful.* Tucson, AZ: Zephyr Press. Chapter 1 is particularly helpful, with detailed information on mock trials and debating at a town meeting. Chapter 3 outlines a history lesson, using a television newscast as the teaching strategy.

Zarnowski, M. & A. Gallagher, eds. 1993. *Children's Literature and Social Studies: Selecting and Using Notable Books in the Classroom.* Dubuque, IA: Kendall/Hunt. This text provides a comprehensive listing of books, many organized thematically. Chapters 10 and 12 focus on curriculum planning. Chapter 4 deals entirely with notable biographies, and Chapter 6 takes the reader to a talk show featuring characters from the past.

References for Writing in Role

Beatty, P. 1987. *Charley Skedaddle.* New York: William Morrow.

———. 1992. *Who Comes with Canons?* New York: William Morrow.

Hunt, I. 1964. *Across Five Aprils.* New York: Follett.

Lyons, M. 1992. *Letters from a Slave Girl: The Story of Harriet Jacobs.* New York: Atheneum Books for Young Readers.

References for Readers Theatre

Poetry for a Civil War Theme

Marius, R., ed. 1994. *The Columbia Book of Civil War Poetry.* New York: Columbia University Press.

Industrialization and Child Labor

Denenberg, B. 1997. *So Far from Home: The Diary of Mary Driscoll, An Irish Mill Girl, Lowell, Massachusetts, 1847.* New York: Scholastic.

Mofford, J., ed. 1997. *Child Labor in America.* Carlisle, MA: Discovery Enterprises.

Weisman, J., ed. 1991. *The Lowell Mill Girls: Life in the Factory.* Carlisle, MA: Discovery Enterprises.

Immigration

Emsden, K., ed. 1993. *Coming to America: A New Life in a New Land.* Carlisle, MA: Discovery Enterprises.

Lawlor, V. (selected and illus.). 1995. *I Was Dreaming to Come to America: Memories from the Ellis Island Oral History Project.* New York: Viking.

Westward Movement

Axelrod, A. (commentary) & D. Fox (arrangements). 1991. *Songs of the Wild West.* New York: Simon & Schuster.

Emsden, K., ed. 1992. *Voices from the West: Life Along the Trail.* Carlisle, MA: Discovery Enterprises.

The Holocaust

Barnouw, D. & G. Van Der Stoom. 1989. *The Diary of Anne Frank, The Critical Edition.* New York: Doubleday.

Brown, J., E. Stephens & J. Rubin. 1996. *Images from the Holocaust: A Literature Anthology.* Lincolnwood, IL: NTC Publishing Group.

Hautzig, E. 1968. *The Endless Steppe.* New York: Harper/Trophy.

Marks, J. 1993. *The Hidden Children: The Secret Survivors of the Holocaust.* New York: Fawcett Columbine.

Meltzer, M. 1988. *Rescue: The Story of How Gentiles Saved Jews in the Holocaust.* New York: Harper/Trophy.

Wiesel, E. 1982. *Night.* New York: Bantam.

References for Storytelling

Asimov, I. 1991. *Christopher Columbus: Navigator to the World.* Milwaukee: Gareth Stevens Children's Books.

Blumberg, R. 1987. *The Incredible Journey of Lewis and Clark.* New York: Lothrop, Lee & Shepard.

Brown, M.M. 1988. *Sacagawea: Indian Interpreter to Lewis and Clark.* Chicago: Children's Press.

Faber, D. 1970. *A Colony Leader: Anne Hutchinson.* Champaign, IL: Garrard.

Ferris, J. 1989. *Arctic Explorer: The Story of Matthew Henson.* Minneapolis: Carolrhoda Books.

Freedman, R. 1996. *The Life and Death of Crazy Horse*. New York: Holiday House.

Fritz, J. 1976. *Bully for You, Teddy Roosevelt*. New York: Putnam.

———. 1991. *What's the Big Idea, Ben Franklin?* New York: Coward-McCann.

Hilts, L. 1987. *Quannah Parker*. San Diego: Harcourt, Brace, Jovanovich.

Kaduto, M.J. & J. Bruchac. 1988. *Keepers of the Earth: Native American Stories and Environmental Activities for Children*. New York: Fulcrum.

Looby, C. 1990. *Benjamin Franklin*. New York: Chelsea House.

McKissack, P. & F. McKissack. 1996. "Cinque and the Amistad." In *Rebels Against Slavery*. New York: Scholastic.

Meltzer, M. 1985. *Mark Twain: A Writer's Life*. New York: F. Watts.

Quackenbush, R. 1986. *Who Let Muddy Boots into the White House? A Story of Andrew Jackson*. New York: Prentice Hall Books for Young Readers.

Scott, J. & R. Scott. 1988. *John Brown of Harper's Ferry*. New York: Facts on File Publications.

Sonneborn, L. 1992. *Clara Barton*. New York: Chelsea Juniors.

Soule, G. 1988. *Christopher Columbus: On the Green Sea of Darkness*. New York: F. Watts.

Villiers, A. 1976. "Magellan: A Voyage into the Unknown Changed Man's Understanding of His World." *National Geographic* 149 (6): 721–53.

Weil, L. 1983. *I, Christopher Columbus*. New York: Atheneum.

The Radio Broadcast

References

Levitin, S. 1970. *Journey to America*. New York: Scholastic.

———. 1989. *Silver Days*. New York: Aladdin/Macmillan.

Sullivan, G. 1991. *The Day Pearl Harbor Was Bombed*. New York: Scholastic.

Resources for Old Radio Show Recordings

Heritage Radio Classics
P.O. Box 16
Chestnut Hill, MA 02167

The Great Radio Shows
304 Eunice Street
Sequim, WA 98382

The Mind's Eye/Memory Lane
P.O. Box 6547
Chelmsford, MA 01824-0947
1-800-227-2020

References for the Poetry/Drama Connection

Brooks, G. 1973. "Martin Luther King, Jr." In *The Poetry of Black America: Anthology of the 20th Century*, ed. A. Adoff. New York: HarperCollins.

Fennessey, S. 1996. *His Name Was Martin: A Play About Martin Luther King, Jr.* Carlisle, MA: Discovery Enterprises.

Holthaus, G.H. 1984. *Circling Back.* Salt Lake City: Peregrine Smith Books.

Hughes, L. 1958. "The Ballad of the Landlord." In *The Langston Hughes Reader.* New York: George Braziller.

———. 1994. "African Dance." In *The Dreamkeeper and Other Poems.* New York: Alfred A. Knopf.

———. 1994. "Merry-Go-Round." In *The Dreamkeeper and Other Poems.* New York: Alfred A. Knopf.

———. 1994. "Frederick Douglass: (1817–1895)." In *The Columbia Book of Civil War Poetry*, ed. T. Marius. New York: Columbia University Press.

Longfellow, H.W. 1990. *Paul Revere's Ride.* (Illus. T. Rand). New York: Dutton.

Reiss, J. 1972. *The Upstairs Room.* New York: Harper/Trophy.

Sitting Bull. 1995. "Behold My Brother." In *Classic Poems to Read Aloud*, ed. J. Berry. New York: Kingfisher.

Whitman, W. 1997. "I Sing the Body Electric (A Man's Body at an Auction)"; "Song of Myself (Come Up From the Fields Father; The Runaway Slave)"; "O Captain, My Captain." In *Walt Whitman*, ed. J. Levin. New York: Sterling.

References for a Television Broadcast

Bober, N.B. 1995. *Abigail Adams: Witness to a Revolution.* New York: Atheneum.

Collier, J. & C. Collier. 1981. *Jump Ship to Freedom.* New York: Dell Yearling

Fritz, J. 1987. *Shh! We're Writing the Constitution.* New York: G.P. Putnam's Sons.

Hautzig, E. 1968. *The Endless Steppe.* New York: Harper Trophy.

Johnston, J. 1973. *They Led the Way: 14 American Women.* New York: Scholastic.

Latham, J. 1955. *Carry On Mr. Bowditch.* Boston: Houghton Mifflin.

Levitin, S. 1970. *Journey to America.* New York: Aladdin/Macmillan.

McGovern, A. 1975. *The Secret Soldier: The Story of Deborah Sampson.* Four Winds Press.

McSwigan, M. 1942. *Snow Treasure.* New York: Apple/Scholastic.

Murphy, J. 1996. *A Young Patriot: The American Revolution As Experienced by One Boy.* New York: Clarion Books.

Selected Resources for the Colonial Museum

Barrett, T. 1995. *Growing Up in Colonial America.* Brookfield, CT: Millbrook Press.

Bracken, J.M., ed. 1995. *Life in the American Colonies: Daily Lifestyles of the Early Settlers.* Carlisle, MA: Discovery Enterprises.

Earle, A.M. 1993. *Child Life in Colonial Days: Books in American Classics Series.* Stockbridge, MA: Berkshire House.

Fisher, L.E. 1965. *The Wigmakers.* New York: F. Watts.

———. 1976. *The Blacksmiths.* New York: F. Watts.

———. 1997. *The Cabinetmakers.* Tarrytown, NY: Benchmark.

———. 1997. *The Doctors.* Tarrytown, NY: Benchmark.

———. 1997. *The Glassmakers.* Tarrytown, NY: Benchmark.

———. 1997. *The Silversmiths.* Tarrytown, NY: Benchmark.

———. 1997. *The Schoolmasters.* New York: Marshall Cavendish.

———. [1973] 1998. *The Homemakers.* New York: Marshall Cavendish.

———. [1971] 1998. *The Shipbuilders.* New York: Marshall Cavendish.

———. [1967] 1998. *The Shoemakers.* New York: Marshall Cavendish.

———. [1966] 1998. *The Weavers.* New York: Marshall Cavendish.

Glubok, S., ed. 1969. *Home and Child Life in Colonial Days.* New York: Macmillan.

Glubok, S. 1970. *The Art of Colonial America.* New York: Macmillan.

Hakim, J. 1993. *Making Thirteen Colonies: History of Us*, vol. 2. New York: Oxford University Press.

Kalman, B. 1991. *Early Schools.* New York: Crabtree.

———. 1992. *Early Travel.* New York: Crabtree.

———. 1993. *Visiting a Village.* New York: Crabtree.

McGovern, A. 1992. *. . . If You Lived in Colonial Times.* New York: Scholastic.

Silverman, J. 1994. *Songs and Stories from the American Revolution.* Brookfield, CT: Millbrook Press.

Tierney, T. 1983. *American Family of the Colonial Era: Paper Dolls in Full Color.* New York: Dover.

Warner, J.F. 1993. *Colonial American Home Life.* New York: Franklin Watts.

6

The Road to Freedom: An Integrated Drama, Social Studies, Language Arts Unit

Drama has taught me how badly blacks were treated when all they wanted was to be as equal as any other man, and it is not until now that I realize how long and violent the road to freedom was for blacks.

William, age 11 (comments taken from an essay in response to a play production)

Like many teachers, I spend the summers reading and planning for the coming school year. I particularly enjoy reading literature related to history, including the latest fiction and biographies for children. One summer I came across the McKissack and McKissack book, *Sojourner Truth: Ain't I a Woman?* While reading, it struck me that the life of Sojourner Truth spanned almost a century (1797–1883). She had experienced slavery before it was prohibited in the North, fought for the freedom of slaves in the abolition movement, witnessed the Civil War, and participated in women's suffrage activities. During her travels, she met many of the noted men and women of her time: Abraham Lincoln, William Lloyd Garrison, Harriet Beecher Stowe, Frederick Douglass, Harriet Tubman, Susan B. Anthony, and Lucretia Mott, just to name a few. This person, I thought, could provide the narrative thread that would help students see the connection in the events leading up to the Civil War.

Planning the Unit

I like using the lives of famous people as a framework for children to develop basic understandings for a time in history. I wanted the students to have an understanding of why the Civil War was fought. They needed to make connections between the knowledge they had already acquired of the past (the slave trade, the Constitution, the development of Northern manufacturing) and the Civil War. I felt that the Sojourner Truth biography would connect the past to the war and its aftermath. With this in mind, I considered the following concepts for the unit:

- Slaves were denied their basic human rights.
- Slavery was prevalent in both the North and the South during Sojourner's early life.
- Abolitionists worked in a variety of ways to stop slavery.
- The pre–Civil War economy was dependent on the slavery sytem, both Northern manufacturing and Southern plantations.
- Slavery was a central issue dividing the country before the war.
- Jim Crow laws denied former slaves their basic rights.

Besides the Sojourner Truth biography, I planned other literature selections as well, books that contained some of the key ideas that would be the focus of instruction. For historical fiction, the choices were *Who Comes With Cannons?* (Beatty), a story revolving around a Quaker family who worked on the Underground Railroad; *Across Five Aprils* (Hunt), which depicts a family and a community divided by war, and *Jayhawker* (Beatty), which recounts the involvement of a young man in an antislavery movement in Missouri. Students picked one to read and discuss in literature group. To the list I added three short biographies to be read by all students: *Sojourner Truth: Ain't I a Woman?*, *The Story of Frederick Douglass*, and *The Story of Harriet Tubman*. In addition to the required reading, there was a list of books that I had identified as helpful to our research. Many of them were in the classroom, and I encouraged students to use them.

Once I had the literature and the historical concepts in mind, I then thought about the strategies that would best complement this unit and my class of diverse learners. I identified skills on which the students needed to work, especially in research, and started planning minilessons that would model a variety of ways for them to present their learning or to outline a particular procedure. The language arts, drama, and theatre strategies that worked well for this unit were the following: writing in role, storytelling, videotape viewing, poetry writing, debating, a living timeline, improvisation, a scripted drama, a Civil War newspaper, journal response, discussion, group and individual research, political cartoons, music, and folk dance. With such a wide array of activities, opportunities were provided for students in all of Gardner's intelligences (see the listing of these activities in Chapter 1).

As I've developed this unit during a number of years, I keep adding and changing the activities, and consequently have accumulated a wide range of choices. I would not try to do all of them in roughly the six weeks I spend on the project, but rather select those that best suit the needs of my kids. Not all students participate in all activities. They sometimes work individually or in small groups. However, the improvisational activities that are outlined in this chapter were designed for participation by the entire class.

The Role the Social Studies Standards Play

During the planning stage for a unit, I also consider the social studies standards. I like to make sure that I'm putting them into practice. With this integrated curriculum approach that employs the arts, literature, reading, writing, and history, there is plenty of opportunity to include them. After reviewing the activities that I typically use to teach this unit, it was evident that the student involvement would easily span all ten strands. These activities would not all be done in this one unit, but I've listed them all here as a way of offering a variety of possibilities. The following sections show how the content and integrated curriculum activities line up with the social studies standards:

I. Culture

Students listen to excerpts from *The Narrative of the Life of Frederick Douglass* and Meltzer's *The Black Americans: A History in Their Own Words*. They *improvise a scene* of a slave auction based on the description in Meltzer's book. They write in role from the point of view of a slave. They *research* the slave culture of the Southern plantation and *learn slave work songs, celebration songs,* and *popular folk dances* of the day. They research period costume for a play production.

II. Time, Continuity, and Change

Students develop arguments for *a debate* between the abolitionists and the Southern planters. They *read historical novels* and consider the different points of view of each historic character and situation. Each literature study group *publishes a Civil War newspaper* from the town in which the book takes place. They examine, through historical novels and primary documents, what life was like for the ordinary person during this time. They consider the differing points of view of Truth and Douglass on how to end slavery. They *create political cartoons* on the issue of slavery/abolitionism and consider the viewpoint being expressed.

III. People, Places, and Environments

Students *examine maps* to locate places where Sojourner Truth lived or traveled on her speaking tours; determine which states were slave, free, or border before the Civil War; and locate settings for each historical novel. They consider the influence of climate on the development of the plantation system and on the types of crops produced, and consider what would have happened to plantations if the labor resource of African slaves had not been available.

IV. Individual Development and Identity

Students *read biographies* of Truth, Douglass, and Tubman, as well as others. They participate in an *improvisation of an abolitionists' meeting* based on accounts detailed in the Sojourner Truth biographies. They consider some of these questions: What was the impact of individuals such as Truth and Douglass on the abolition of slavery? What were examples of their courageous behavior? How would you have behaved in a similar situation? Why do accounts of a person's life differ from biographer to biographer? How did these people change in the course of their lives? How can we reconstruct important events in Truth's life? What events should be a focus? How much detail should be included? How are we behaving like historians by presenting a play about her life? What do each of you need to do to help us accomplish our goal of presenting a play about Truth's life?

V. Individuals, Groups, and Institutions

Students prepare and *present a living timeline* after reading biographies and researching the abolitionists, as well as other famous people of the time. They *view a videotape of the Underground Railroad*. They consider the following questions: What was the role of the abolitionists in bringing about the end of slavery? What influence does each particular individual have on the events that led up to the Civil War? Besides the Underground Railroad, what other forms of resistance were waged by slaves against their owners?

VI. Power, Authority, and Governance

After reading the biographies, students look at the Bill of Rights. They consider the following questions *in a class discussion:* How were slaves denied their basic human rights? What was the result of slaves not being granted their freedom at the writing of the Constitution? What was the effect of the Supreme Court decision in the Dred Scott case? How did the Constitution change after the Civil War? They *view excerpts from the videotape of Roots, Episode 2.*

VII. Production, Distribution, and Consumption

Students *research* pre–Civil War slavery in the South and consider the following questions in a class discussion: What was the impact of slave labor on cotton and tobacco production in the South? What was the connection between Northern manufacturing and Southern slavery? How did the Civil War affect the South's supply of manufactured goods from the North? How did the war affect established transportation systems? Students *view a videotape* (Episode I) of Ken Burns' Civil War series to help them understand the importance of the plantation system in the pre–Civil War economy.

VIII. Science, Technology, and Society

After researching the plantation sytem, students discuss the following questions: What effect did the invention of the cotton gin have on the institution of slavery in the South? What were the similarities and differences between the factory system in the North and the slave system in the South? They *participate in a town meeting* taking place in a Northern manufacturing town where abolitionists and anti-abolitionists air their differences over factory conditions and the slave system.

IX. Global Connections

After researching and reading the biographies, students consider the following questions in a *class discussion*. How did the Fugitive Slave Law promote emigration of slaves to Canada and other countries during the pre–Civil War period? What was the impact of the Civil War on international trade?

X. Civic Ideals and Practices

Students *participate in an improvisation* based on Sojourner Truth's attempt to integrate the trolley system in Washington, DC. After the *presentation of a full-length scripted drama* on Truth's life, students consider the following questions in class discussion: How did Sojourner Truth's beliefs effect change in her life as well as others'? How was Sojourner Truth able to use the court system to her advantage when trying to have her son returned from the South, and when trying to secure the integration of the trolley system in Washington, DC? By what means did Truth present her Land Grant Plan to Congress? How can you apply what you've learned in this unit to your life as a citizen in this school, your town or city, our country, and the rest of the world?

Organizing with a Model

I depend on the drama/theatre activities to be the motivating force that keeps students actively involved in the pursuit of learning. The literature is also a central component in the curriculum. From these readings, students have a common ground for discussion and a knowledge base upon which to draw when portraying characters in a timeline, improvisational, and scripted drama, or when preparing material for a debate or newspaper. To organize the planning and to visually show the options that I might use for this unit, I developed an interdisciplinary curriculum web. This model, shown in Figure 6–1, represents my attempt to indicate how the arts can be an integral component in a literature-based social studies curriculum.

Initiating the Topic with a Drama Experience

When I want to get my kids interested in a topic, I rely on drama to motivate them. For this project, I planned an improvisational drama of a *slave auction* for their first experience. After the students were gathered in the drama area, I brought out the Milton Meltzer book, *The Black Americans: A History in Their Own Words,* for a read-aloud of the section "A Slave Auction 1841." I posed the question, "What is an auction?" Many responded by telling me about furniture or paintings that go up for sale and that people bid on them. A few said that they had been to auctions with their parents. I told them that I would be reading about an auction and I directed them to listen to find out what "goods" were being sold.

After the reading, we discussed the content and recorded pertinent information on chart paper to provide plot ideas for the scene. It looked something like this:

- Slave men were arranged on one side of the room and slave women on the other.
- Slaves were given specific places to stand in line.
- Before the sale, they practiced parading to and from places with exact precision.
- Slaves were made to dance the Virginia Reel for the customers.
- Slaves were closely examined and felt by the customers.
- A slave couple was purchased by one man.
- A slave boy, Randall, was sold separately from his mother.

The read-aloud also provided suggestions for characters, some with specific names. There were parts for everyone in the class. Our character list looked like this:

- Freeman, owner of the slave pen
- male slaves
- female slaves
- customers
- Bob, the fiddle player
- Solomon, a slave
- David and Caroline, slave couple
- Randall, slave boy
- Eliza, Randall's mother
- a planter from Baton Rouge

Setting was also discussed, and it was agreed that as each slave went up for sale, they would be elevated on a small platform or box. This idea came from a drawing of a slave auction seen in the Meltzer book.

After the parts were chosen, we began the scene. The first time through the improvisation, we focused on the exhibition or parade of slaves for the planters. In subsequent sessions, we worked on the auction and the separation of mother and child. Each session was followed by a teacher-led discussion (the method of questioning is described in Chapter 3). The scene became more detailed. Several weeks

Topic: Slavery/Abolitionism

Social Studies Concepts

- Slaves were denied their basic human rights.
- Slavery was prevalent in both the North and the South during Sojourner's early life.
- Abolitionists worked in a variety of ways to stop slavery.
- The pre–Civil War economy was dependent on the slavery system, both Northern manufacturing and Southern plantations.
- Slavery was a central issue dividing the country before the war.
- Jim Crow Laws denied former slaves their basic rights.

Literature

Fiction
Who Comes with Canons?
Across Five Aprils
Jayhawker

Biography
Sojourner Truth: Ain't I A Woman?
The Story of Frederick Douglass
The Story of Harriet Tubman

Writing Skills

- Write responses to the biographies read.
- Respond to novels in literature group.
- Write an article for the Civil War newspaper.
- Write poems about slavery, Sojourner, and Jim Crow laws.
- Create slave auction posters.
- Write in role as a slave.
- Write to report findings in research.

Reading Skills

- Read and discuss novels in a teacher-guided literature group.
- Read biographies independently.
- Research topics: slavery in the North, pre–Civil War slavery in the South, slave culture on the plantation, slave resistance, slaves in the Civil War, the abolition movement
- Create a living timeline ranging from Sojourner's birth to her death after the Civil War.

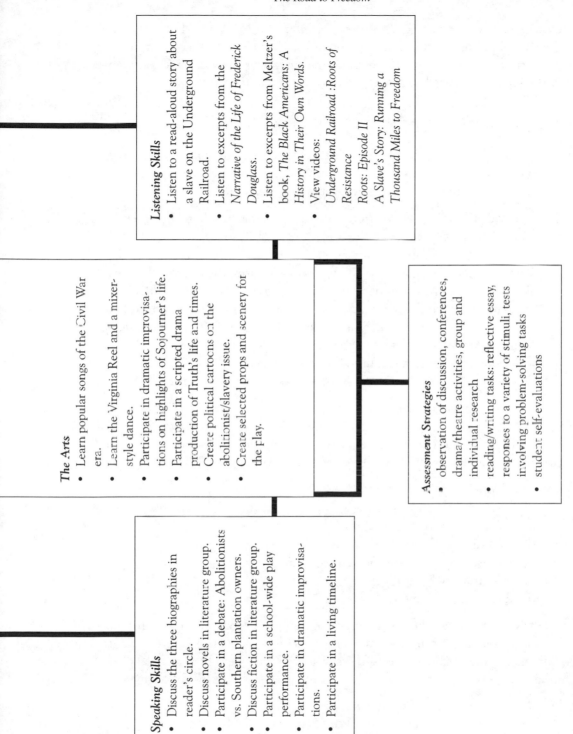

Listening Skills

- Listen to a read-aloud story about a slave on the Underground Railroad.
- Listen to excerpts from the *Narrative of the Life of Frederick Douglass.*
- Listen to excerpts from Meltzer's book, *The Black Americans: A History in Their Own Words.*
- View videos:
  Underground Railroad : Roots of Resistance
  Roots: Episode II
  A Slave's Story: Running a Thousand Miles to Freedom

The Arts

- Learn popular songs of the Civil War era.
- Learn the Virginia Reel and a mixer-style dance.
- Participate in dramatic improvisations on highlights of Sojourner's life.
- Participate in a scripted drama production of Truth's life and times.
- Create political cartoons on the abolitionist/slavery issue.
- Create selected props and scenery for the play.

Speaking Skills

- Discuss the three biographies in reader's circle.
- Discuss novels in literature group.
- Participate in a debate: Abolitionists vs. Southern plantation owners.
- Discuss fiction in literature group.
- Participate in a school-wide play performance.
- Participate in dramatic improvisations.
- Participate in a living timeline.

Assessment Strategies

- observation of discussion, conferences, drama/theatre activities, group and individual research
- reading/writing tasks: reflective essay, responses to a variety of stimuli, tests involving problem-solving tasks
- student self-evaluations

Figure 6–1. Integrated Social Studies/Drama/Language Arts. Topic: Slavery/Abolitionism

later, when students had read the biography of Truth, they learned that she, too, had been sold at an auction and separated from her parents. Sojourner, named Isabelle Hardenbergh, eventually became the subject of the slave auction scene, with the separation from her Ma-Ma Bett as the dramatic focus.

Organizing for Research

With the students now excited about the subject matter, the next step was to get ready to learn more about the subject. Before the investigation began, there were several steps I took to give students an overview of the topic:

1. I provided readings that briefly summarized the problems between the North and the South before the war.
2. I shared more read-alouds with the entire class.
3. We started building a timeline on the board, putting the birth of Sojourner Truth on one end and her date of death on the other, and then added a few other dates for which we already had information. Each date and explanatory phrase was written on eight-by-eleven-inch pieces of tagboard and attached by magnets to the blackboard. In the following weeks, more dates were added that were relevant to the main topic (examples: 1827, New York State officially frees slaves; 1850, the Fugitive Slave Law is passed).

I then assigned students a research topic, grouping them according to my assessment of their various intelligences and levels of social development. The topics were directly related to the literature and essential to the realization of the culminating project, a play on the life of Sojourner Truth. The groups investigated the following subjects:

- slavery in the North
- pre–Civil War slavery in the South
- slave culture on the plantation
- slave resistance, including the Underground Railroad
- slaves in the Civil War
- the Abolition Movement

Students were encouraged to use a variety of resources. Many of them were available in a special area of the classroom set up with books (some of them picture books), maps, and cassette tapes. Others were found in the school or local public libraries. Some of the books that were particularly useful were the following:

Abraham Lincoln and the End of Slavery by Russell Shorto
The Black Americans: A History in Their Own Words by Milton Meltzer
Break Those Chains at Last: African Americans, 1860–1880 by Noralee Frankel

Daily Life on a Southern Plantation, 1853 by Paul Erikson

Days of Slavery: A History of Black People in America by Stuart Kallen

Dear Friend: Thomas Garrett and William Still, Collaborators on the Underground Railroad by Judith Bentley

Escape from Slavery: Five Journeys to Freedom by Doreen Rappaport

Frederick Douglass: Voice of Liberty by Melissa Banta

Get on Board: The Story of the Underground Railroad by Jim Haskins

Go Free or Die: A Story About Harriet Tubman by Jeri Ferris

Harriet Beecher Stowe and the Beecher Preachers by Jean Fritz

Harriet Tubman: Slavery and the Underground Railroad by Megan McClard

A History of Us: Liberty for All? vol. 5 by Joy Hakim

A History of Us: War, Terrible War, vol. 6 by Joy Hakim

A History of Us: Reconstruction and Reform, vol. 7 by Joy Hakim

If You Traveled on the Underground Railroad by Ellen Levine

John Brown: Militant Abolitionist by Robert L. Potter

Let My People Go: African Americans, 1804–1860 by Deborah Gray White

Lincoln: A Photobiography by Russell Freeman

Lucretia Mott: Friend of Justice by Kem Knapp Sawyer

A Nation Torn: The Story of How the Civil War Began by Delia Ray

Nettie's Trip South by Ann Turner

North Star to Freedom: The Story of the Underground Railroad by Gena Gorrell

Ordinary Americans: U.S. History Through the Eyes of Everyday People edited by Linda Monk

Our Song, Our Toil: The Story of American Slavery as Told by Slaves by Michele Stepto

Rebels Against Slavery: American Slave Revolts by P. McKissack and F. McKissack

Slavery in the United States, Jackdaw No. A30 compiled by William Hine

Sojourner Truth: Ain't I a Woman? by P. McKissack and F. McKissack

Sojourner Truth and the Struggle for Freedom by Edward Beecher Claflin

Sojourner Truth: Anti-Slavery Activist by Peter Krass

Sojourner Truth: Crusader for Civil Rights by Norman Macht

The Strength of These Arms: Life in the Slave Quarters by Raymond Bial

Til Victory Is Won: Black Soldiers in the Civil War by Zak Mettger

The Underground Railroad: Life on the Road to Freedom by Ellen Hansen

Voices from the Civil War by Milton Meltzer

Walking the Road to Freedom: A Story About Sojourner Truth by Jeri Ferris

Minilessons to Help with Research

Before the first research session actually began, I presented a minilesson to review research skills. The first lesson reminded students to start with some basic questions:

What do we know about our topic? What do we want to know? How can we learn more about it? When the research was underway, the minilessons continued for the purpose of facilitating the research activities and making my expectations clear. The following minilesson topics, I have found, are helpful to the students.

How Do You Take Notes?

This lesson modeled the process by looking at a relevant piece of historical information on a transparency and deciding what was important and how to write it down.

How Do You Find the Information You Need?

In this hands-on lesson, students browsed through many books to review the usefulness of the table of contents, index, glossary, chronology of events, sidebars, pictures, and captions for getting information about the topic.

What Did You Learn and How Can You Share It?

This lesson was taught in three sessions because three different book formats were presented as choices for reporting what they had learned during their research. Each group, I explained to them, was expected to present their research in an illustrated book. (Although there are many ways to present research, both orally and in writing, for our purposes, in this particular project, a traditional book format was used.) They had a choice of three styles:

1. first-person narrative, as in a letter or diary
2. a question-and-answer book
3. an informational-style chapter book

After listening to all three minilessons, the group had to decide which format would best suit their topic. As I presented each of the minilessons, I explained that some topics might lend themselves naturally to a particular style of presentation.

In the first minilesson, *first-person narrative*, I used the picture book, *Nettie's Trip South*, by Turner, as the model. This book uses a letter as a device. It starts with "Dear Addie" and ends with "Love, Nettie." In between, the author uses the letter of this young Northern girl to her friend as a way to reveal the horrors of the institution of slavery in the South. The book is short enough to be incorporated into the lesson as a read-aloud.

For the second minilesson, I presented the *question-and-answer book* format. This was modeled with the picture book, *If You Traveled on the Underground Railroad*, by Levine. This book, after a short introduction, has one question on each page, with an answer and an illustration. This straightforward style attracts many students as a way to present research.

The focus of the third lesson was an *informational-style chapter book*. Erikson's *Daily Life on a Southern Plantation, 1853*, was used as the model. I showed the minichapters in this picture book, pointing out other features, such as maps, illustrations, a timeline, and a glossary. I encouraged all groups, regardless of the format they chose, to include a glossary, a timeline or chronology of events, and a bibliography for the reader.

The books were finished in about four weeks and were shared with the entire class in a presentation. Afterward, they were displayed in the classroom, to be used as a resource for other individuals.

Reading the Biographies and Responding in Writing

Each student read three biographies during this unit (see Figure 6–1). Sometimes I opt to have them read only one, depending on how much time I have to devote to the project. I have found that it is possible to do three if I have biography selections at varying reading levels. In the project being described, for example, not all students read *Sojourner Truth: Ain't I a Woman?* Some read a sixty-four-page biography by Jeri Ferris, *Walking the Road to Freedom*. I allow a week or more for each biography, and then the students rotate books. The more advanced readers will finish a biography in a day. Other readers might take the entire time allowed. By the end of three or four weeks, the students have read all three biographies and have responded in writing to each. Students use a set of guidelines to prepare the response (see model in next section). The questions posed in the guidelines help students organize their thoughts as they write expository paragraphs, as well as formulate their own opinions on the subject. I also suggest that students use a timeline to show the significant events in the person's life. This is my attempt to avoid the type of response that is a long narrative, listing every event in the person's life, connected with a series of "then he . . . ." From the timeline, I encourage students to pick out only the most important events that made the person noted in history and write about those.

Sample Guidelines for a Biography Response

After reading the biography:

1. Create a timeline to show the sequence of significant events in the person's life.
2. Ask yourself this question: What event(s), beliefs, actions, or writings made the person famous in history? Write about these highlights only. (Do not retell the person's entire life.)
3. Ask yourself these questions: What do I admire about the person? Do I

agree or disagree with any of the person's ideas? Support your answer with examples.

4. Create an illustration that captures the person in action. Give your illustration a caption (a descriptive title under the illustration).

Additional Activities Connected to the Biographies

After reading and responding to the three biographies, the students had a solid knowledge base that was put to use in a wide range of activities. Without a firm knowledge base, I find that the kids are limited in their level of participation. These activities included *discussion, writing in role, debating,* and a *living timeline.*

Discussion

During *discussions* with the entire class (we called it "readers circle"), they were able to compare and contrast the lives of the three abolitionists. They considered such questions as the following: In what ways did each abolitionist work to end slavery? How did their views differ? What did their writings reveal about the treatment of slaves? Who were other famous abolitionists working at this time? Did everyone in the North agree with the abolitionists' views? How did abolitionists in the South conduct their antislavery activities?

Writing in the Role of a Slave: Two Variations

As mentioned in the section on *writing in role* (Chapter 5), students are highly motivated to write when assuming the character of another person. I used this strategy for several reasons in the Sojourner Truth unit: first, to help students realize that slaves were real people with feelings, not just a name in a book, and second, to help them assume the role of a slave in the play with more depth and understanding.

After participating in the slave auction improvisation (described earlier in this chapter), reading the biographies, researching, and listening to read-aloud excerpts from *Letters from a Slave Girl,* students were beginning to formulate a picture of what life was like for a Southern slave. For one writing activity, I gave each student a copy of a poster advertising a slave auction in 1835. The advertisement listed all of the male and female slaves who were for sale, along with their ages, a description, and job experience. (Example: "Sarah, a mulatress, age 45 years, a good cook and accustomed to housework in general, is an excellent and faithful nurse for sick persons and in every respect a first rate character.") We read the poster together, discussing and clarifying the content. After the discussion, I told students to pick one of the slaves listed, and assuming the role of that person, write a diary entry(ies) either just before or just after the slave auction took place. From our research, students were aware that most slaves had not been taught to read or write because it was prohibited by law. The direction for the writing activity was as follows: "If these slaves could write, what thoughts might they put in a diary either before or after the slave auction?" What follows is one student's response to the poster. She addresses her diary entry to "North Star" and purposely misspells a number of words.

Dear North Star,

I was goin' to be awcshoned next. Mary Ann, a girl I guess about my age, had been seperted from her family, sold for $450 to Master Brown. He said he'd whip her good if she didn't behave herself. Mary Ann cried and cried, so he whipped her good to make her stop. I wanted to cry myself, but I didn't dare. It was my turn. The Awcshoner pulled my arm and forced me out on the platform. "Intelligent, quick, name's Emma." Then the awcshoner made me run across the platform to demonstrate. My legs ached and I couldn't run that fast. The awcshoner hit my legs with the whip to make me go faster, like one does to a horse. It made me shiver inside and feel mighty uneasy. "Ten or eleven years of age, good at sewing and waiting on a table, an orphan", the awcshoner went on, making me turn and lift up my shirt to show how few scars were on my back. I felt like dirt, to them I was less than even the cattle. I was lower than the pigs. They didn't care if I died, or if I spit up blood. The only care they had was that they woodn't get as much money for me, or that I wood get the blood on their fancy clothes and such. I wanted to cry out, scream, change things. But I remained silent, knowing my only way out was to follow you to freedom, but how? There was no time to think about that, then I heard the people's voices calling out loid, "50 dollars!" one man shouted. "70 dollars!" another man shouted. "90 dollars!" said another. "150!" "200!" "260!" "320!" "400!" the bids kept up until "750! going once, twice, three times . . . sold!"

Yours truly,

Emma

P.S. I'm coming.

Chelsea, age 10

A variation of this writing activity involved the use of the Sojourner Truth biography. After reading the biography, I told students to imagine that they were in the shoes of Sojourner as she worked as a slave on farms in New York, frequently being sold from one owner to another. Then I asked, "If you were writing her diary, what would her entries reveal about her experiences as a slave?"

A Debate: Abolitionists Versus the Southern Planters

In Chapter 5, I made suggestions on how to prepare the class for a debate, stressing the importance of researching and preparing arguments. For this debate topic, few students wanted to argue the case for the Southern planters. So, before the debate teams were chosen, we did some brainstorming. Recording on the overhead projector, we came up with good arguments for both sides. By doing this, students could see that it was possible to build a good case for the plantation owners. We did this activity in a couple of short minilessons, with short assigned readings as well as small group discussion in between each session. This generated more ideas for the second brainstorm session. Finally, arguments for both sides were listed, after which, students decided which role they wanted to play: an abolitionist or a Southern planter. The brainstorm lists looked something like this:

Abolitionists Might Argue

Slaves have no rights, they're not free. They're forced to work without pay.

Declaration of Independence declared that "All men are created equal."
Southern laws prevent slaves from getting an education. They can learn if given a chance.

Owners don't protect slaves, they abuse them. They are fed like animals, whipped, made to work from sunrise to sunset. They often sleep on floors in unheated cabins. Only 4 slaves in a hundred live to be 60.
No one has the right to own another human. One out of seven Americans are enslaved.

Southern Planters Might Argue

The Constitution didn't guarantee their freedom. If they were free, how would they support themselves? They're not educated and not smart enough to care for themselves.
Slaves are inferior to whites in every respect, not equal.

Slaves are happy the way they are.

They sing while they work, show no interest in books.
We must feed, clothe, house, protect, and care for them. What would they do without us? They don't have the skills to earn a living.

We didn't start slavery. It's been in this country since the 1500s. Why change now? Slavery has helped the country grow and the South grow. Without slave labor, our cotton production will falter. We won't be able to supply the huge demand of the Northern mills. We wouldn't need so many slaves if Northerners didn't demand so much cotton.

Conditions in mills are bad, but workers are free. They are paid. Slaves should bepaid for their labor. Planters are greedy. Your mansions and luxuries are supported by the labor of your slaves.

Slaves are better off than workers in the Northern mills. Many work outdoors where the air is clear. We purchased our slaves, spent good money, and we take care of our property. Why should we give it away? Northern states have no right to determine our laws here in the South.

After the two debate teams were formed, they worked to develop more arguments, both logical and emotional. (These were informal teams, half the class on each team, not according to formal debating rules.) During this time, they also created individual character autobiographies. By imagining a character, students were better able to portray a point of view and argue with conviction during the debate. A variety of characters emerged, some quite detailed, with specific mannerisms, accents, and backgrounds. This activity firmly established the real or imagined character in the mind of the debater.

A Living Timeline of Sojourner Truth's Contemporaries

We were well into the unit when students prepared for the living timeline. They had read the biographies, done related reading, and participated in discussion and improvisation. During these activities, the names of famous people living at the time of Sojourner Truth surfaced. Students were alerted to the fact that we would be doing a living timeline, and they were on the lookout for an interesting character to portray. They were eager to prepare for this activity, and for weeks I heard the names of famous historic people whispered around the room.

The living timeline was similar to the description given in Chapter 5. Students created a short autobiography for their characters (performed as a one- to two-minute monologue), emphasizing the highlights of each person's life. With this timeline, however, there was one added feature: Each character had to make reference to Sojourner Truth, stating how they personally knew her or had heard of her, and how they felt about her abolitionist work. Because Truth's life spanned so many years, our list of character choices was easily created. The appendix in *Sojourner Truth: Ain't I a Woman?* was a very helpful resource, listing people that Sojourner knew, with a short biography of each. The list of choices from which the students picked was as follows:

Male Characters

Richard Allen, former slave/abolitionist

Frederick Douglass, former slave/abolitionist

John Brown, militant abolitionist

William Lloyd Garrison, abolitionist/publisher

John Jay, chief justice/abolitionist

David Ruggles, abolitionist/publisher

Abraham Lincoln, U.S. president

Ulysses S. Grant, U.S. president/general

Joseph Cinque, African/slave

John Calhoun, senator

Charles Sumner, senator

Jefferson Davis, Confederate president

Robert Gould Shaw, colonel,
54th Massachusetts Regiment

Thomas Garrett, active in the
Underground Railroad

Wendell Phillips, abolitionist/writer/
speaker

Dred Scott, slave

Stephen A. Douglas, senator

Robert E. Lee, Confederate general

Henry Clay, senator

Daniel Webster, senator

Walt Whitman, poet

Anthony Burns, fugitive slave

John Greenleaf Whittier, poet

Female Characters

Susan B. Anthony, abolitionist/
women's rights activist

Elizabeth Stanton, women's rights
activist

Harriet Beecher Stowe, writer/
abolitionist

Frances E.W. Harper, poet/abolitionist

Sarah Grimke, abolitionist/women's
rights activist

Elizabeth Blackwell, doctor

Lydia Marie Child, abolitionist

Sarah Emma Edmonds, spy/soldier

Ellen Craft, escaped slave

Lucretia Mott, abolitionist/women's
rights activist

Lucy Stone, women's rights activist

Harriet Tubman, former slave/
abolitionist

Mary Lyon, educator/women's rights
activist

Angelina Grimke, abolitionist/women's
rights activist

Julia Ward Howe, writer/abolitionist

Louisa May Alcott, writer

Dorothea Dix, equal rights activist

Rebecca Harding, activist for rights of
the laborer

Publishing a Newspaper as a Response to Historical Fiction

Literature plays a central role in an integrated unit such as this. The biographies
were a springboard for activities such as a debate, a living timeline, and writing in
role. The historical fiction selections and the literature group meetings were also a
key component, adding to the students' knowledge base in history and language
arts. All of the readings, both fiction and nonfiction, paved the way for the following project: publishing a newspaper that was a combination of fact and fiction.

During the Sojourner Truth unit, literature group meetings were held regularly
with three different groups: *Across Five Aprils, Jayhawker, Who Comes with Canons?*

In addition to the literary elements of plot, character, setting, mood, and theme, we also discussed the historical content of the books. After completing the reading of the books, each group published a newspaper as a group project.

The newspaper is a format enjoyed by intermediate and middle grade students. They assume the role of various types of reporters and editors, covering national and local news, weather, obituaries, births, marriages, community events, letters to the editor, political cartoons, and editorials. Classified and product advertisements also are included. If students haven't had experience with newspaper writing, I teach a few introductory lessons. I schedule several during writing and reading times. During the first lesson, we look at the *format of a newspaper* and the types of stories it contains. In a separate session, I show reprints of newspapers published around the time of the Civil War. The classified ads are fun to read, and the print looks strange to children who are used to modern newsprint. In the second lesson, we examine a news article to determine if the standard questions of newswriting are answered: *who, what, when, where, why,* and *how.* The title of the third lesson is *fact and opinion,* focusing on the difference between a news article and an editorial or political cartoon. Some children this age, I find, have difficulty separating fact from opinion, and although I conference with them during the writing of their news stories, opinions still slip into the news articles. Briefly stated, it's important to prepare students for this activity, and although I haven't detailed many aspects of newspaper writing here, this topic is explained thoroughly in many language arts textbooks and other literature for teachers.

For these newspaper projects, students were directed to accomplish the following:

- Create a newspaper located in the town that was the main setting of the book. Example: For *Who Comes with Canons?*, the story took place in Goldsboro, North Carolina, so the group created a newspaper called *The Goldsboro Times*
- Include local news stories connected to the book's plot. Example: A local news story for the *Across Five Aprils* newspaper, *The Newton Gazette,* featured a story about the wounding of Shadrach Yale (one of the leading characters in the book) at the battle of Gettysburg. The following is a sample of a student's piece of writing.

Newton Comes Close to Losing a Teacher

Christopher (age 10)

The local schoolteacher Shadrach Yale got badly injured in a recent battle at Gettysburg. He is now in the hospital in Washington, D.C. When he gets back, he probably won't be teaching for awhile.

Jenny Creighton, daughter of Matthew Creighton, went up to Washington, along with Ross Milton, to check on Shadrach. Shadrach had been sent to Washington so he could be with his aunt, a nurse, instead of coming all the way back to Newton.

- Include stories of current national events. This involves research. Students need to check a variety of sources, such as a timeline book, encyclopedias, and textbooks, for story ideas and information. Example: The *Jayhawker* group in a newspaper dated October 18, 1859, headlined with a story about John Brown's Raid on Harper's Ferry. The *Goldsboro Times*, dated April 16, 1865, ran a story on the assassination of President Lincoln. The *Newton Gazette*, dated July 16, 1863, featured an account of the battle of Gettysburg. Sample excerpts of this story are included here.

  Lee's Army in the North

  Tom, age 11

  On July 1, 1863, General Robert E. Lee and his troops invaded the north to capture the supplies the southern army needed. Luckily General Mead and his Union boys were in the area of Gettysburg to stop them.

  . . . The battle went on for two more bloody days. Although Mead's army was hard hit, nothing could compare with the massive casualties Lee's army endured. Canon booms and battle cries were heard all over the state of Pennsylvania those three days. . . .

- Include editorial opinions, political cartoons, and letters to the editor. Example: *The Newton Gazette* reflected a Northern point of view in an editorial about the battle of Shiloh, while a political cartoon, reflecting a Southern viewpoint, appeared in the *Goldsboro Times* and is shown here in Figure 6–2.

Students were creative with the content of the newspapers. Inspired by plot material in their historical fiction books, they included items such as a social events calendar, obituaries, birth and marriage announcements, interviews with a wounded soldier and a general, seasonal recipes, classified ads, and profiles of famous people.

Computers were used to type the articles in newspaper format; then they arranged the order of the articles, along with any drawings they wanted to include, cutting and pasting when needed. The result was three different newspapers, one for each literature group. Enough photocopies were made for the entire class to share in the reading.

Figure 6–2. A Civil War–Era Political Cartoon Reflecting a Southern Viewpoint

In the Spotlight: The Creation of a Scripted Play

This section is a description of the components that contributed to the creation of the scripted play, *The Road to Freedom,* a culminating activity for the unit. Earlier in this chapter, I focused on the importance of the core literature, the research, and the accompanying activities that paved the way for the final production.

In the Spotlight begins with a focus on the creative drama activities that were incorporated into the scripted drama. The "Slave Auction," described earlier, was the opening scene of the play, in which Isabelle Hardenbergh (Sojourner Truth), at age eleven, is sold at an auction. Another scene in the play, which began as a drama/social studies lesson, was based on an incident that took place on a trolley car in 1863. An outline for the lesson and the scene material follows.

The Trolley Car Incident

> When the street car stopped, I ran and jumped aboard. The conductor pushed me back saying, "get out of the way and let this lady come in." "Whoop," said I, "I am a lady too."

Sojourner Truth

Sojourner worked as a nurse in refugee camps in Washington, DC after slaves were freed. One day, as she was coming back from work at a hospital, she showed her determination to integrate the segregated trolley cars by attempting to board one.

Source of Inspirational Material

Sojourner Truth and the Struggle for Freedom, by Edward Beecher Claflin (Chapter 11, "Freedom Rider")

Historical Understanding

After the Emancipation Proclamation, former slaves were still denied their basic civil rights.

Ideas Revealed Through the Source Material

- Trolley cars were segregated.
- The Freedman's Bureau was designed to help former slaves make the transition from slavery to freedom.
- Sojourner Truth used the court system to help integrate the streetcar system in Washington, DC.

Beginning the Drama Session

After reading aloud an account of the trolley car incident, we discussed, then outlined the event.

Scene Outline: The Trolley Car, Washington, DC (1863)

> *Who:* Sojourner Truth, Mrs. Laura Haviland (Sojourner's friend and philanthropist), the conductor, white passengers on the trolley
>
> *Where:* A trolley car in Washington, DC
>
> *What* (the scenario created from the situation and characters presented in the source material and developed during creative drama sessions): Sojourner Truth and Mrs. Haviland are waiting at the trolley, exhausted after their day working in the hospital. The trolley stops and Sojourner tries to board. The conductor orders her to make way for the woman behind her (Mrs. Haviland). Both women argue with the conductor. Passengers are outraged that a black woman wants to board a "white" trolley. The argument gets worse, the conductor pushes Sojourner and she falls, dislocating her shoulder. They leave the trolley, headed back to the hospital.

The Abolitionists' Meeting

> I have ploughed and I have planted. And I have gathered into barns. And no man could head (beat) me. And ain't I a woman?

> Sojourner Truth

Another drama session in class produced a scene for the play called "The Abolitionists' Meeting." This, too, was inspired by the literature and evolved to the performance level after several sessions. Truth spent more than thirty years of her life trying to end slavery, lecturing in the Northeast and Midwest, becoming known as a stirring and inspirational speaker. I used this information and two chapters in the McKissacks' book as source material for this scene. An outline for the lesson and the scene material is shown here.

Source of Inspirational Material

Sojourner Truth: Ain't I a Woman? by McKissack & McKissack (Chapters 7 and 8)

Historical Understanding

Women's rights and the emancipation of slaves were two causes being fought at the same time.

Ideas Revealed Through the Source Material

- Sojourner and some abolitionists supported the cause of the women's rights group.
- Men came to women's rights meetings to protest, trying to keep women from speaking.
- Sojourner made it clear, through her speeches, that racism and sexism were unacceptable.
- Frederick Douglass, who held a long-standing nonviolent position, changed his stance to support violence as a solution to the slavery issue. Sojourner was unwilling to accept Douglass' opinion, and maintained a nonviolent approach.

Beginning the Drama Session

After the students had read the Sojourner Truth biography, I reviewed two chapters that detailed her experiences as a speaker. We discussed the content. Through my questioning, we focused on the conflicting ideas of several factions. At antislavery society meetings, there were often anti-abolitionists who opposed the group's ideas and came to heckle the speakers. In some of Sojourner's audiences, men who were opposed to women's rights came to protest the female speakers, creating a hostile situation. These conflicts became the core ideas for the following creative drama session.

Scene Outline: The Abolitionists' Meeting

Who: Sojourner Truth, Frederick Douglass, men and women at the meeting
Where: Akron, Ohio (1851)
What (the scenario created from situations and characters presented in the biography): Frederick Douglass is at the podium speaking about the emancipation of slaves, advocating violence, if necessary. An anti-abolition group heckles him. The chairman intervenes, confronting them and eventually ejecting them from the meeting. The chairman then introduces Sojourner. As she approaches the podium, a group of male protesters calls out, trying to prevent her from speaking because she is a woman. She begins her talk and is interrupted by a woman, who demands, "What has women's rights to do with abolition?" Sojourner continues, addressing this issue in her famous "Ain't I a Woman?" speech. More questions and protests come from the audience, and Sojourner answers them fearlessly. By the end of her talk, she has the audience laughing and applauding.

The Integration of Music and Dance into the Script

Music and dance were woven into the framework of the script, conveying a mood and time period. For example, while reading the firsthand account of a slave auction in the Meltzer (1964) book, we learned from Solomon Northup that slaves were often forced to dance as a way to show their physical well-being: "After being fed, in the afternoon, we were paraded and made to dance." Further reading reveals that the dance was the Virginia Reel. The students mastered this simple folk dance quickly, but its incorporation into the scene, "Slave Auction," required additional thought. I asked more questions: "How do you think this dance was performed at a slave auction? Did the dancers face the buyers? What mood prevailed? How would you feel about dancing if you were being sold? Could you show your true feelings? What would the auctioneer expect from the slaves' dance?"

Again, from the Solomon Northup account, I learned that Christmas was one of the few holidays for slaves. They were given a day or two off, with extra food and passes to visit relatives. This information provided an idea for another scene in the play, "Christmas in the Slave Quarters." In it, Belle (Sojourner) announces the news that all slaves in the state of New York will be freed on July 4, 1827. Hearing this, the holiday party becomes a joyous celebration, culminating in the singing of the folk song "Cindy," and the performance of a mixer-style folk dance.

In the final scene, two popular Civil War–era songs set the tone for "The Union Army Campground, Thanksgiving 1863." Sojourner and some of her friends bring food baskets to the 1st Michigan Black Infantry. Before they arrive, the soldiers are gathered around the campfire singing, "Johnny Is My Darling." As the scene closes, Sojourner sings a song that she composed especially for this black infantry, sung to the tune of "The Battle Hymn of the Republic."

> We are the hardy soldiers of the First of Michigan;
> We are fighting for the union and for the rights of man.
> And when the battle wages you'll find us in the van,
> As we go marching on.
>
> We are the valiant soldiers who 'listed for the war;
> We are fighting for the union, we are fighting for the law.
> We can shoot a rebel further than a white man ever saw,
> As we go marching on.
>
> They will have to pay us wages, the wages of their sin;
> They will have to bow their foreheads to their colored kith and kin;
> They will have to give us house-room, or the roof will tumble in,
> As we go marching on.

Creating Props and Scenery

I have found that it is important for young actors to assume some of the responsibility for the preparation of the artistic elements of the production. It demonstrates the amount of time and effort necessary for the preparation of props and scenery, and allows students to employ their visual intelligences. Ideally, students should prepare all the scenery for a production, but from my experience, this is not practical for the following reasons: First and most importantly, there is not enough time in the normal schedule of a school day; second, many intermediate or middle grade students have not yet developed the artistic or social skills to handle such a responsibility, and, as stated in Chapter 4, the director has the responsibility to make the production the best quality possible with the resources available. (Simply prepared scenery is acceptable, but sloppily painted scenery detracts from a play production.) My solution is participation on a limited basis. Small groups of students prepare one or two special items (examples: broadsides for the slave auction, posters to advertise the play) or several simple pieces of scenery (examples: painting the boxes used for platforms in the slave auction, making a papier-mâché tree stump). For such activities, I give students clear directions and supervise them carefully.

Costumes

Costuming this production required a little research to determine men and women's styles of the early and mid-1800s. The intent was to suggest a particular style rather than imitate it in detail. The boys wore dark trousers and plain shirts. Ankle-length skirts and white blouses were worn by the girls. To these basic costumes, aprons, shawls, bonnets, hats, vests, coats, and ties were added when appropriate. An inexpensive felt infantry hat was ordered from a company in Pennsylvania (see Resources) for the scene at the Union Campground. In the same scene, the girls wore "poke" bonnets. These were sewn by several parent volunteers.

The Scripted Play

Most of the scripted play was created from scenes developed in the creative drama sessions in class. They were scenes involving the entire cast in some instances and almost all students in others. They were the following scenes:

- Scene 1: The Slave Auction
- Scene 4: The Slave Quarters on Christmas Eve
- Scene 7: The Abolitionists' Meeting
- Scene 8: The Trolley Car in Washington, DC
- Scene 9: The Union Army Campground

The remaining scenes and narration, which I wrote, involved only three or four actors on stage at once. These scenes highlighted the most dramatic events of Sojourner's life, such as her escape from the slave master John Dumont. A sample scene is included here.

Scene 6: The Escape to the Quaker Family

(Narrators are onstage as the lights come up. The scene is set for the Quaker house.)

NARRATOR: Isabelle finally realized that Dumont thought nothing of breaking a promise to a slave.

NARRATOR: She made plans to run away.

NARRATOR: She knew she wouldn't get very far with five children, and was forced to leave them behind with other slaves, all except Sophie.

NARRATOR: She decided she would go as soon as she finished spinning the annual harvest of wool.

NARRATOR: Just before dawn in October, she quickly made a bundle of clothes and food,

NARRATOR: took Sophie in her arms, and quietly set off for the farm of a Quaker family, the Van Wagener's.

(Belle enters and runs across stage with the baby in her arms, then mimes knocking at the door of the house. Mrs. Van Wagener opens the door.)

ISABELLE: Mrs. Van Wagener, I'm Isabelle, the Dumont's slave. I've been running since sun-up. I can't run another step. My baby is tired and hungry and . . .

MRS. VAN WAGENER: (interrupting) Come in, Isabelle. Thou art welcome in this house.

MR. VAN WAGENER: What has happened to thee? Why are thee running away?

ISABELLE: It's Mr. Dumont, sir. He broke his promise. He told me that I could go free. Then when the fourth of July came, he said "No," said he didn't recollect his promise, said I didn't work hard enough. But, that ain't true. I worked day and night, did the job of two slaves.

MRS. VAN WAGENER: We believe thee, Isabelle. Thou may stay in our house as a free woman.

MR. VAN WAGENER: We will give thee a job. My wife could use some extra help here in the house.

ISABELLE: Oh, thank you, sir. You are both so very kind.

MRS. VAN WAGENER: Here, let me take thy baby. Thou must be exhausted from carrying her all day.

(There is a loud banging at the door. Dumont is yelling)

DUMONT: Let me in. I know she's in there. Belle! I know you're there. (Mr. Van Wagener opens the door and Dumont struts past him and heads toward Isabelle.) I knew you'd be here. Why did you run off in the night like that?

ISABELLE: I didn't run away, I walked away, and it was daylight too!

DUMONT: You come with me right now or you'll be whipped, like you've never been whipped before. You're *my* property, I'm *your* master, and *you're* coming with me!

MR. VAN WAGENER: Mr. Dumont, my wife and I have offered Isabelle a job, and a home, and she has agreed to stay with us. As for being *her master*, I disagree. There is but one Master. He is my Master, Isabelle's Master, and Mr. Dumont, he is *your* Master.

DUMONT: Well, *this* master is taking her home. (He steps forward to grab Isabelle, and Mr. Van Wagener steps in between. Dumont threatens with his gun.) Step aside, Van Wagener, I'm not afraid to use this.

MR. VAN WAGENER: I'm not afraid of thee. A gun won't solve this problem, or any problem. Put it away , Mr. Dumont.

DUMONT: I *said*, step aside!

MR. VAN WAGENER: If it's money thee want, I'll pay thee for Isabelle, and her daughter. Here, take this. (He reaches in his pocket and pulls out some money.) There's $25.00. She's never going to go back with you anyway. And, even if she does, she's not going to work the way she did before. Thee might as well have something. Take the money.

DUMONT: (reaches out and takes the money) All right, but this is *not* the end of it. You'll be sorry you left, just you wait. (heads out the door and turns) Just you wait, Belle! You'll be sorry. (He exits.)

MRS. VAN WAGENER: Isabelle, thou has had a very busy day. Let me show thee to thy bed. (The Van Wagener's show Isabelle a small benchlike bed.) Thou can sleep here by the fireplace. I'll put the baby in the crib in our room. Goodnight, Isabelle.

ISABELLE: Goodnight, Mrs. Van Wagener, and thank you for the kindness you've shown me.

(*Mrs. Van Wagener exits. Isabelle stares at the bed for awhile, then finally curls up on the floor and goes to sleep. The lights fade briefly to indicate a passage of time, then the lights come up again, and Isabelle rises, stretches, goes to check the fire, and Mrs. Van Wagner enters.*)

MRS. VAN WAGENER: Good morning, Isabelle. (pauses and looks at the bed) Thou didn't go to sleep last night?

ISABELLE: Yes, I never slept better.

MRS. VAN WAGENER: But thou hasn't been in thy bed!

ISABELLE: Mrs. Van Wagener, I never been in a bed in my whole life. It never came to my mind that you meant for me to sleep in it, did you?

MRS. VAN WAGENER: Of course, Isabelle. (chuckling) Thou are not a slave any more. Why shouldn't thee sleep in a bed?

(*There's a knock at the door*)

Who could that be? I'm not expecting anyone. (crosses to the door) Who is it?

LIZZIE: It's Lizzie! I'm a slave o' Master Dumont. I need to talk to Belle.

MRS. VAN WAGENER: (opens the door) Thou are welcome in my house.

ISABELLE: Lizzie, what are you doing here? If Mr. Dumont finds out, you'll be whipped.

LIZZIE: I know, but I had to see you. Mr. Dumont done somethin' terrible. It's about Peter, your son Peter.

ISABELLE: What's happened?

LIZZIE: He was so angry when you run away that he sold Peter south, to a man from Alabama. He's gone to a cotton plantation.

ISABELLE: Oh, no! Not Peter, gone south, he's only a child. What can I do? (pause) What will become of him . . . . . . on a plantation!!

MR. VAN WAGENER: What's all this commotion? What has happened?

MRS. VAN WAGENER: John Dumont has sold Isabelle's son to an Alabama planter.

MR. VAN WAGENER: Why, he can't do that. It's against the law. New York forbids slave owners to transport their slaves out of state.

LIZZIE: You mean Master Dumont broke the law?

MR. VAN WAGENER: Yes, and Isabelle can file a lawsuit against him, bring him to court, and hopefully get her son back.

LIZZIE: Oh my! Would I like to see that! Mr. Dumont brought to court! (turning to Belle) Belle, I best be going before the Master finds out. I sure hope you get little Peter back. Bye, Belle. And good luck!

ISABELLE: I'll have my child again, don't fear. The Lord will help me get him back.

(Lizzie exits. Isabelle and the Van Wageners exit the opposite side. Narrators enter.)

NARRATOR: So Isabelle went from house to house, asking for donations from Quaker friends. She managed to collect enough money to hire a lawyer.

NARRATOR: A Grand Jury heard Isabelle's case and decided in her favor.

NARRATOR: Isabelle walked proudly out of the courtroom with Peter.

NARRATOR: With only courage and determination, she had become one of the first black women in the country to win a court case.

(Blackout)

Figure 6–3. Students Perform in *The Road to Freedom.* RIC Office of News & Public Relations, Gordon Rowley, Photographer

Assessment

Each student in my class has a portfolio in which a variety of artifacts are stored. Early in the school year, students are familiar with the word *artifacts*. I introduce the term in a lesson called, "How do historians find out about the past?" They also participate in an activity called "Artifacts" and "Artifacts II" (both described in Chapter 2). They understand that artifacts are evidence from the past. So when I use the word *artifacts* to describe the evidence of learning experiences that they are collecting for their portfolios, they easily understand it.

What Artifacts Are in the Portfolio?

For this particular unit on slavery/abolitionism, the artifacts collected during the six- to eight-week unit might be the following. (Note: Not all of the activities listed would be in a typical portfolio. The contents depend on those activities selected by the teacher for the unit, and best suited for the class.)

- a student self-evaluation (see Chapter 2)
- a social studies/drama teacher observation checklist (see Chapter 3)
- student research notes, draft, and final copy of cooperative research project
- diary entries, written in the role of a slave (see Chapter 6)
- an audiotape of a one-minute monologue (biography for the living timeline), or written script (see Chapter 6)
- introduction and outline of arguments for a debate (see Chapter 6)
- three biography responses of Truth, Douglass, and Tubman (see Chapter 6)
- a response journal for one of the three historical fiction choices in literature discussion group (see Chapter 6)
- a published copy of the Civil War newspaper created for a literature group project (see Chapter 6)
- a written response to the play, *The Road to Freedom* (see Chapter 6)
- a videotape of the play production (one copy stored in the teacher's portfolio)
- a written test that incorporates the conceptual material in the unit (see Chapter 6)

Oral and Written Responses to the Play Production Experience

After the culminating play production, I set aside time to discuss with the students the whole experience of the preparation and performance of the play. We discuss it in drama circle. The feedback is often quite astonishing, surprising me with comments about what they've learned or experienced. Other remarks are predictable. For example, most all realize that teamwork is the most important factor in a successful performance. Later, I have students put their comments in writing, asking them to consider the following open-ended question: What have you learned from your participation in the play project (for example, about history, theatre, yourself)? Students always have a lot to say. As I read their comments, I evaluate them for evidence of the social studies concepts and indicators of social development. The following are excerpts of responses written after *The Road to Freedom* production.

I think I learned how cruelly (cruelly) people were treated just because of the color of their skin. I also learned that all people should be treated with respect. . . . Also about the important things Sojourner did for her country, and without her and the other abolitionists, there still might be slavery today.

Matthew, age 11

I learned a lot about slavery, more than I probably ever have, especially since I had the experience of being a slave.

Leah, age 11

Being in a play takes really hard work and dedication. I used to "boo" at plays when I didn't like something, but now I don't because I know they put a lot of time into it.

Shawn, age 11

Being in the play helped me know that if you put a lot of effort into something, it's worth it. It also added to my self-confidence. And I'm not afraid of a big audience (audience) any more.

Carter, age 10

Some things I learned about history were shocking to me because I never really had thought about how people were treated back then, especially slaves. But now, after learning about many abolitionists (Truth, Douglass, Tubman, and Garrison etc.) I think I could safely say that nobody in this class or the other classes in the school, really had thought about why they (abolitionists) were famous, or how bad it was being a slave, or the long journey they went through to be free. Now I know, and the experience will help me remember when I get older that color, religion, or age doesn't matter.

Sarah, age 11

The concern of the abolitionists toward slavery caught me and I noticed how far they would go to abolish slavery. . . . Working together is the most important thing when putting on a play. If you don't get there together, then you can't get there.

Sam, age 11

I also learned that working with others is 99% of the whole play. If you can't cooperate with everyone in the play, your whole play is pretty much thrown away.

Lindsay, age 10

I learned that in the early 1800's slavery was still leagal (legal) and thousands of African Americans were owned and forced to work on plantations. They were sold like cattle at auctions and were beaten by their masters. They were also traded for rum.

Stephanie, age 11

Learning about this stuff was both fun and serious. I learned the basic way of life back then. Seeing it from both views, an abolitionist's point of view, and also a planter's point of view. It was interesting and sad to see how some people were treated and sometimes slotered (slaughtered).

Christian, age 11

I gained confidence and some good friends, and it felt good when I did the play because I felt independent and I felt like I could do anything.

Samuel, age 10

A Written Test

A unit test is another artifact that I include in the student's social studies portfolio. I create a test that combines short answers and essays. I find that this combination allows most learners the opportunity for success. There are often those students who have difficulty organizing and expressing their thoughts in writing. Although, with the experiential approach described in this chapter, I've observed that most students, if not all, have a clear understanding of the big ideas and seem to have less difficulty with essay-style questions. A selected sample of questions that I have used for the Slavery/Abolitionists Unit is included here for the purpose of illustration.

- Imagine you are attending a debate on the issue of slavery. Speaking against slavery is the abolitionist, Sojourner Truth. Speaking in favor of slavery is a rich cotton plantation owner. He produces cotton to sell to Northern manufacturers and he owns several hundred slaves. What might be some arguments that you would hear from each side?
- It's 1852 and you are a field slave working on a cotton plantation in Alabama. If you could write, how would you describe your living and working conditions on the plantation? Write your description in a letter to a friend in the North.

Resources

Selected Professional Resources

Berlin, I. & S. Miller, eds. 1998. *Remembering Slavery: African-Americans Talk About Their Personal Experiences of Slavery and Emancipation.* New York: The New Press/Norton. This book is a compilation of transcribed audiotapes recorded in the 1930s. Former slaves, who were interviewed as part of the Federal Writers' Project, give accounts of their years in slavery, which are poignant and sometimes horrifying. This book gives a very human face to slavery. Select stories with the age of your students in mind.

Fennessey, S. 1997. *The Road to Freedom: A Play About Sojourner Truth, Slave and Equal Rights Activist.* Carlisle, MA: Discovery Enterprises. This is a play with nine scenes that span Sojourner's slavery days to her nursing work in Civil War refugee camps. There are parts for 25+ male and female speaking roles.

Hart, D. 1994. *Authentic Assessment: A Handbook for Educators.* Reading, MA: Addison Wesley Innovative Learning. Hart's is a very helpful book for those who are interested in learning some of the basics about authentic assessment. It explores the issues of tailoring assessment to desired outcomes and scoring, and evaluating student performance.

Lindquist, T. 1997. *Ways That Work: Putting Social Studies Standards into Practice.* Portsmouth, NH: Heinemann. This is a very practical resource that models different ways that social studies content can be organized in elementary and middle schools, and presents a wide assortment of strategies to help you do it. Chapter 1 makes the case for using historical fiction, nonfiction, and primary sources in the teaching of social studies. It also explains how to plan a cooperative unit.

Meltzer, M., ed. [1964] 1984. *The Black Americans: A History in Their Own Words, 1619–1983.* New York: HarperCollins. African American men, women, and children reveal what they thought, felt, and did through their letters, diaries, journals, autobiographies, speeches, and court testimony. Especially helpful for a unit on slavery are "Slavery Days," "A Slave Sale," "Christmas on the Plantation," "It Was a Glorious Day!", and "To My Old Master."

Silverman, J. 1996. *Just Listen to This Song I'm Singing: African-American History Through Song.* Brookfield, CT: Millbrook Press. Along with this collection of musical scores for voice and instrument, Jerry Silverman writes an introduction that gives a brief history of slavery. A detailed narrative explains the significance of each song.

Resources for Costumes

Kalman, B. 1993. *Historic Communities: 19th Century Clothing.* New York: Crabtree.

To order Civil War infantry hats, contact:

> Servant & Company
> Centennial General Store
> 230 Steinwehr Ave
> Gettysburg, PA 17325
> (717) 334-9721

Literature for the Unit on Slavery

Core Literature (fiction and biography)

Beatty, P. 1991. *Jayhawker*. New York: Beechtree.

Beatty, P. 1992. *Who Comes with Canons?* New York: Scholastic.

Hunt, I. 1964. *Across Five Aprils*. New York: Berkley/Pacer.

McKissack, P. & F. McKissack. 1992. *Sojourner Truth: Ain't I a Woman?* New York: Scholastic.

McMullan, K. 1991. *The Story of Harriet Tubman, Conductor of the Underground Railroad*. New York: Dell/Yearling.

Weiner, E. 1992. *The Story of Frederick Douglass, Voice of Freedom*. New York: Dell/Yearling.

Literature Useful for Research Topics on Slavery and the Civil War

Altman, S. & S. Lechner. 1993. *Followers of the North Star*. Chicago: Children's Press.

Banta, M. 1993. *Frederick Douglass: Voice of Liberty*. New York: Chelsea Juniors.

Bentley, J. 1997. *Dear Friend: Thomas Garrett & William Still, Collaborators on the Underground Railroad*. New York: Cobblehill Books.

Bial, R. 1997. *The Strength of These Arms: Life in the Slave Quarters*. Boston: Houghton Mifflin.

Blockson, C.L. 1984. "Escape from Slavery: The Underground Railroad." *National Geographic* 166 (1): 3–39.

Claflin, E.B. 1987. *Sojourner Truth and the Struggle for Freedom*. (Henry Steele Commager's Americans) New York: Barron's Educational Series.

Douglass, F. 1968. *Narrative of the Life of Frederick Douglass, An American Slave*. New York: Signet/Penguin. (Original work published 1845)

Erikson, P. 1997. *Daily Life on a Southern Plantation, 1853*. New York: Lodestar/Dutton.

Ferris, J. 1988. *Go Free or Die: A Story About Harriet Tubman*. Minneapolis: Carolrhoda Books.

———. 1988. *Walking the Road to Freedom, A Story About Sojourner Truth*. Minneapolis: Carolrhoda Books.

Frankel, N. 1996. *Break Those Chains at Last: African-Americans, 1860–1880*, vol. 5. New York: Oxford University Press.

Freedman, R. 1987. *Lincoln: A Photobiography*. New York: Clarion Books.

Fritz, J. 1994. *Harriet Beecher Stowe and the Beecher Preachers*. New York: Putnam.

Gorrell. G. 1997. *North Star to Freedom: The Story of the Underground Railroad*. New York: Delacorte.

Hakim, J. 1994. *A History of Us: Liberty For All?* (Book 5). New York: Oxford University Press.

———. 1994. *A History of Us: War, Terrible War* (Book 6). New York: Oxford University Press.

———. 1994. *A History of Us: Reconstruction & Reform* (Book 7). New York: Oxford University Press.

Hansen, E., ed. 1993. *The Underground Railroad: Life on the Road to Freedom.* Carlisle, MA: Discovery Enterprises.

Haskins, J. 1993. *Get on Board: The Story of the Underground Railroad.* New York: Scholastic.

Hine, W., ed. 1975. *Slavery in the United States, Jackdaw No. A-30.* Amawalk, NY: Golden Owl.

Kallen, S. 1990. *Days of Slavery: A History of Black People in America 1619–1863.* Minneapolis: Rockbottom Books.

Krass, P. 1988. *Sojourner Truth: Antislavery Activist.* New York: Chelsea House.

Levine, E. 1988. *If You Traveled on the Underground Railroad.* New York: Scholastic.

Macht, N.L. 1992. *Sojourner Truth: Crusader for Civil Rights.* (Junior World Biographies). New York: Chelsea Juniors.

McClard, M. 1991. *Harriet Tubman: Slavery and the Underground Railroad.* Englewood Cliffs, NJ: Silver Burdett.

McKissack, P. & F. McKissack. 1996. *Rebels Against Slavery: American Slave Revolts.* New York: Scholastic.

Meltzer, M., ed. 1989. *Voices from the Civil War.* New York: Harper Trophy.

Mettger, Z. 1994. *Till Victory Is Won: Black Soldiers in the Civil War.* New York: Puffin Books.

Monk, L.R., ed. 1994. *Ordinary Americans: U.S. History Through the Eyes of Everyday People.* Alexandria, VA: Close Up Publishing.

Potter, R. 1995. *John Brown: Militant Abolitionist.* Austin, TX: Raintree/Steck-Vaughn.

Rappaport, D. 1991. *Escape from Slavery: Five Journeys to Freedom.* New York: HarperCollins.

Ray, D. 1996. *A Nation Torn: The Story of How the Civil War Began.* New York: Puffin Books.

Sawyer, K.K. 1998. *Lucretia Mott: Friend of Justice.* Carlisle, MA: Discovery Enterprises.

Shorto, R. 1991. *Abraham Lincoln and the End of Slavery.* Brookfield, CT: Millbrook Press.

Steins, R. 1993. *The Nation Divides: The Civil War 1820–1880.* (First Person America). New York: Twenty-First Century Books/Henry Holt.

Stepto, M. 1994. *Our Song, Our Toil: The Story of American Slavery As Told by Slaves.* Brookfield, CT: Millbrook Press.

Turner, A. 1987. *Nettie's Trip South.* New York: Aladdin.

White, D.G. 1996. *Let My People Go: African Americans 1804–1860,* vol. 4. New York: Oxford University Press.

Useful Videotapes for the Unit on Slavery

Bagwell, O. (producer). 1990. *Roots of Resistance: A Story of the Underground Railroad* [videotape]. Boston: WGBH.

Burns, K. & R. Burns (producers). 1992. *The Civil War: Episode 1, The Cause* [videotape]. Chatsworth, CA: Image Entertainment, Inc.

Margulies, S. (producer). 1992. *Roots, Episode 2* [videotape release of 1977 television miniseries]. Burbank, CA: Warner Home Video.

Schlessinger (producer). 1992. *Black Americans of Achievement Video Collection: Sojourner Truth* [videotape]. Bala Cynwyd, PA: Schlessinger Video Productions, a Division of Library Video Co.

Resources for the Play Production

Music

McNeil, K. & R. McNeil. 1989. *Civil War Songs with Historical Narrative.* Riverside, CA: WEM Records.

Silverman, J. 1993. *Ballads and Songs of the Civil War.* Pacific, MO: Mel Bay Publications.

———. 1994. *Slave Songs.* New York: Chelsea House.

———. 1994. *Work Songs.* New York: Chelsea House.

Traugh, S. 1994. *Voices of American History,* vol. II. *The Young Nation Through the Civil War.* Cypress, CA: Creative Teaching Press.

Addresses:

> WEM Records
> 16230 Van Buren Boulevard
> Riverside, CA 92504
> (909) 780-2322
> Fax (909) 789-0130

> Mel Bay Publications, Inc.
> #4 Industrial Drive
> Pacific, MO 63069-0066

To obtain the Smithsonian Folkways catalogue of historical folk recordings, write to:

> Smithsonian Folkways Recordings
> Center for Folklife Programs & Cultural Studies
> 955 L'Enfant Plaza, Suite 2600
> MRC914
> Washington, DC 20560
> 1-800-410-9815
> Http://www.si.edu/folkways

To obtain folk dance recordings and dance directions, contact:

> Folk Arts Center of New England, Inc.
> 1950 Massachusetts Avenue
> Cambridge, MA 02140
> (617) 491-6083 or 491-6084

7

The Curtain Never Closes on Learning

As a classroom teacher, I'm always beginning something new, never quite the same as the year before because it has evolved as I observe, reflect, and make changes in my practices. Planning is never really finished. As a novice teacher, I thought that if I grabbed a history unit prepared the year before, my planning was already done. That wasn't so. Adjustments, I discovered, were always needed. Now I know better, and accept the fact that my new class of learners will have different needs and talents than the class before. My thinking, too, has changed as I learn from observing my students, attending conferences, and reading and sharing ideas with colleagues. As I gather and test new knowledge in my classroom, I ask myself what works for my students. I recognize that unlike the theatre, where the closing curtain signals the end, the process of learning for a teacher or student is ongoing. The teaching strategies that I've shared in this book work for me and my students, but as they are put into practice, they might need to be adjusted to fit individual teaching styles, students' needs, and the classroom situation.

The Constants: Attributes for Successful Classroom Practices

Although, from year to year, my teaching changes, there are some constants that are the infrastructure of my practices. I've made a list here of those behaviors that foster a productive, cooperative spirit in the classroom.

- It is important to have a sincere respect for all learners, an acceptance for who they are as individuals and what they can do academically. When children sense my respect for them, they respond with openness, reacting as they truly are—curious, creative individuals.
- It is crucial for me to show that I believe in what I do, exhibiting an honesty and openness with my kids. If I'm enthusiastic about using drama and theatre as a teaching strategy, the learners are motivated, recognizing my

169

passion for the subject. It's not something I can fake. Children intuitively know a faker. They see it in the eyes and the body language.

- I try to be flexible. Even though I plan a unit and daily lessons, it doesn't mean that those plans can't change. As the unit unfolds, and I sense what my students need to learn, I adjust accordingly. An activity that was successful with last year's class might not work with this year's class. I might need to modify it, expand it, or abandon it altogether. I listen to the ideas that the kids have to offer and utilize them whenever possible.

- It's difficult at times to have courage to experiment, but courage is needed. Those not familiar with learning through the dramatic arts might be critical, thinking that I run a noisy, undisciplined classroom. On the contrary, the arts require lots of self-discipline. I've learned also from experience that if the strategy helps the kids learn, I use it. I don't wait for reassurance from others. For example, I take a risk when I write plays and we share them with a school-wide audience. My students take a similar risk when they perform, or simply share their writing with me or their peers in the classroom. Courage is needed to participate in the theatre games or improvisations, but if I expect my kids to join in, then I should be willing to risk involvement as well.

- I try to maintain an attitude of patience with my students and myself. Change takes time. If I'm presenting a new activity in improvisational drama, for example, it takes a while for the kids to feel comfortable with it. If students haven't previously experienced learning in this way, it will take them some time to build their skills in drama. There are no shortcuts when it comes to planning and learning, so I've learned to relax. It takes time to plan an integrated unit, time to carry it out, and time (maybe three or four years) to make it really work smoothly. It also takes time for students to absorb the content, for example, of a theatre production. I try not to rush the process, because I believe that there is great value to learning in an in-depth fashion. The students have the time to experience history. I have time to observe and listen to them.

- I find that it is essential to set and maintain high standards for myself and my students. If I don't put much thought and energy into my teaching, then I can't expect the kids to do so. For students, high expectations include academic performance and social behavior. I try to choose topics that will interest and challenge them, and utilize methods aimed at unlocking the potential in every student, promoting creative thinking, discovery, and problem solving. I also strive to interact with the kids in a way that encourages cooperation and discipline.

The Variables: Modeling, Conferencing, and Discussion

Just as there are aspects of my teaching that rarely change, there are also those that change with regularity. These variables have to do with the methods I employ in classroom instruction. I change them often, picking and choosing those that suit my students' needs and the situation. I use a variety of them, but they can be grouped into the three general types of practice that I've presented with examples throughout this book:

1. *Modeling*. Through minilessons, I present an idea, give examples to demonstrate the idea, and sometimes practice the new skill with the students. I do it often. When students are shown how to do something, they are better able to do it on their own. For example, for the minilesson in Chapter 6 called, "What did you learn and how can you show it?", students were shown three formats for presenting research writing. Afterward, they were clear about my expectations.

2. *Conferencing*. I conference with individuals and small groups. The questions I pose during interactions facilitate learning. I do conferencing often. The more conferences I conduct with students, the better the results. (For example, conferencing during various stages of a research project is essential.) Conferencing can also take the form of "side coaching" (modeled in Chapter 3), those comments made while students are engaged in a drama activity.

3. *Discussion*. Discussion is a practice that I mention often in this book. I use it especially when the entire class is involved in improvisational drama. Good questioning skills are central to the success of this activity. I try to pose questions that encourage an understanding of the lesson's content, help students put ideas into context, and see their relationship to other ideas. I encourage students to engage in meaningful discussion, and develop their ability to state opinions, reflect, and listen respectfully (see Figure 3–2, Observation Checklist).

Experimenting with Drama and Theatre in the Social Studies Classroom

In the Preface, I expressed my hope that teachers reading this book would be inspired to try some of these ideas in their own classes. These practices have worked for me, and I'm confident that they'll work for others. While I plan and experiment with these activities, I keep in mind that they are a vehicle for the content and not a substitute, providing a different and exciting way for students to learn about history. The drama and theatre practices alone will not create historically literate students. Rather, it is a combination of elements. The way I interact with my students is an important component. The methods I use (the minilessons, modeling, conferencing, discussions) are another factor. The content and the way it's presented also contribute to successful learning. With all three working in harmony, the social studies classroom is an exciting place. I've never had a student who didn't want to be involved in our drama or theatre projects. The following comments express the excitement felt by two students when writing about their experience in a play about the life of Langston Hughes, *Hold Fast to Dreams.*

> The lights dimmed. This was it. Time to go on. In a jumble, we walked out on stage. The lights grew brighter and brighter. They grew so bright, I could hardly keep my eyes open. "Get used to it", I told myself, knowing we still had an hour of performing to do. The music to *Hold Fast to Dreams* came on. I started to sing, knowing that my mom, dad, neighbor, the two fourth grades, one sixth grade, and one third grade were in the audience along with what seemed like 400 moms and 83 dads with Panasonic taperecorders.

Nick, age 10

> In the play, I experienced Langston's life. I learned many things from it and it was an easier way to learn stuff for me. Then to replay his whole life for someone else was something. Just being on stage excited me, but then I was being a teacher to kids younger and some older. It was great.

Brian, age 11